HOW WE ARE HEALED

Finding God's Help When You're Hurting

By
JEFFREY DRISCOLL

PRESS

www.xulonpress.com

May 2009

Mason,

Thank you for your help with our business. I appreciate your dedication and expertise in audiology practice!

God bless you!

Jeff Driscoll

ECC 5:18-20

Preface

This book is intended as a quick reference and resource guide to help people who are struggling with difficult situations in life.

Table of Contents

Section 1 – Why Are We Here?

Chapter 1 – Questions We All Ask.

Is there a God? Where did the universe come from? How did life begin? Is there a purpose for my life? These are universal questions nearly every child asks. Is it just curiosity? As teenagers, we become so self-centered that we couldn't care less about these questions. But at some point in our life, perhaps in college, or later, often in the depth of a crisis, they take on a new and more mature importance. They have been answered by scientists and theologians as accurately as possible with the information we have built over our 6000+ years of human history. As more information becomes available, or new theories are posited and tested, we get a more focused view of human history and our origin. We also find out what information is accurate, and what is inaccurate.

The universe is made up of both physical and spiritual components. When scientists attempt to explain the physical universe apart from theology, they are tying half their brain behind their backs. To insist that there must be a physical explanation for everything flies in the face of logic and experience. On the other hand, to explain the universe as anything but physical, that it is all an illusion, ignores the reality of the physical laws of matter and energy that we observe. Most people see the folly in that, yet it has been proposed. We cannot explain the human mind, or even locate where the mind resides in the body. We cannot explain where thoughts come from, but we experience and use these throughout our lives. Yet, we can't dismiss that which we physically experience through philosophical foolishness either. If there is a non-physical component to our universe, then physical science alone can never explain that component. Scientists who insist that the explanation for the universe and the origin of life can be any answer except God err by eliminating the only correct answer. When we begin with a false assumption, we cannot find the true answer. And, if there really is a God, then He would have been the One to create the physical laws of the universe, and we would find complete harmony between theology and scientific observation. The physical and spiritual universe are both very real, neither can be discarded if the truth is to be fully understood. And they work together in harmony according to a Master Plan.

Physical science alone has not satisfactorily answered the question concerning the origin of life. Theories of a primordial soup "creating" living cells from proteins, enzymes and DNA or RNA are speculative at best, having never had any success in any relevant laboratory experiments. We have not had any success at creating life from non-living elements. Even setting the origin of life aside and considering Darwin's Theory of Evolution as a possibility to explain humans' evolving from single-celled life forms over millions of years has been completely debunked. It has been proven impossible for all practical purposes. The fossil evidence has not yielded a single transitional example of one species becoming a completely different species, when there should be millions of examples if the theory is valid. Darwin himself admitted if the fossil evidence did not support his theory, then the theory was dead.[a] We certainly observe adaptation of species and variations within a species, but not transitional forms. The Cambrian Explosion actually opposes what would be expected to be observed by Darwin's theory. Our observations of the entire universe simply do not fit the Theory of Evolution. Darwinian evolution is flawed science. We observe intelligent design. We find DNA as the blueprint of life. DNA is information, just like a computer software code. DNA can only lose information, it never gains information by any natural process. We see order moving toward disorder, the opposite of evolution. There are physical laws that govern our physical universe. The laws of thermodynamics govern the inter-relation between heat, work and internal energy of a system. The First Law of thermodynamics basically states that energy in the universe is constant, it can not be created or destroyed, it can only be changed from one form to another (energy is conserved). The Second Law of thermodynamics (also called the Law of Entropy) states that everything moves toward equilibrium because of entropy (order always becomes disorder; disorder never becomes order) The Third Law says that there is a lowest temperature, called absolute zero, where entropy is zero. This temperature can be calculated, but it is impossible to attain.

I like what British scientist and author C.P. Snow had to say about the three laws:

You cannot win (that is, you cannot get something for nothing, because matter and energy are conserved).

You cannot break even (you cannot return to the same energy state, because there is always an increase in disorder; entropy always increases).

You cannot get out of the game (because absolute zero is unattainable).[b]

Let's take it a step further. If we take a recently deceased human, all of the elements of a person are there, but there is no heartbeat, no brain activity, no respiration, no life. We do not have the technology or ability to make that person live again, no matter how much we rebuild, transfuse, or electronically coerce that which is dead. We can not raise the dead back to life. We can't even repair many forms of disease or paralysis from brain and spinal injuries in people who are alive, or repair partially dead body parts damaged from frostbite, gangrene or other diseases requiring amputation to prevent the whole organism from dying. Once the spirit is separated from the body, we can not rejoin them, only God can do that. These are the physical and spiritual laws that govern our world and they are woven together.

So, how did the universe begin? A Big Bang? Possibly. The Bible says that God created everything from nothing. That sounds like it could fit what has been described as the Big Bang theory. But someone still had to cause the Bang. Our Laws of Physics require the intervention of an outside source when there is an eternally stable mass that suddenly begins expanding to become the universe we observe. Stephen Hawking has calculated the equation of the universe backward to within a nanosecond (~10 to the -43rd power, Planck time) after the Big Bang at which point the theory breaks down.^{c} That would be near the point at which the mass is stable, not expanding or contracting, not exchanging heat or light. What caused this stable mass to suddenly begin expanding to become our universe? Did it already exist, or did it suddenly appear out of nothing? The point at which the theory breaks down could be the point at which the mass was brought into existence. Did Hawking discover the mathematical point of Creation? There had to be a Creator of the Bang. The late Carl Sagan stated he did not see any reason to pursue the origin of the universe to the point of answering the question, "What caused the bang?" I don't think he wanted to know the answer while he was alive, but I suspect he has met the Answer by now.

And how did life begin? Modern science has no provable answers, only a theory or two that require outside intervention to substantiate. The Bible tells us life was created by God. God spoke into existence all of the plants, birds and animals. God created Adam from the earth and God breathed the breath of life into Adam. There is no evidence to refute that, and the time frame certainly fits known human history. The chemical makeup of humans also fits the Biblical account. So, the Bible adequately explains how the universe began, how life began, and that there is a God, and it fits with what we observe and calculate. This is 3000 year old genius on such an incredible level, that if it were not information from God, no human could possibly know this or write it with such accuracy as to be irrefutable. All human theories can be tested and if not proven true, at least be discarded as impossible. Any human who had come up with such genius, also would have taken credit for it, and would be world renowned, like Plato or Socrates. Yet, the Bible gives the credit to God. Hmmmm.

What about our purpose? If we were created, there must have been a purpose for creating us. There are people who have spent their entire lives looking for some purpose, some depth of meaning. It is undisputed that if there is no God, then there is no meaning to life, it is all completely accidental. So when an atheist searches for the meaning of life, he makes the same mistake as the scientist who eliminates God and can never discover the correct answer, he has already eliminated it. There is no reason to search for meaning in that which is meaningless. Only the person who is open to the possibility of the existence of God has the ability to find an answer to the meaning of life. That is because it is God who gives meaning to life!

The Bible tells us that God created us for relationship with each other and with Him. He only created one man and a woman from that man, and then He told them to populate the world. He gave them the ability to reproduce and to become caretakers of the planet He created for them to live on. He created humans to bring honor and glory to Himself. He created the universe so that we would marvel at who He is, and how unfathomable His abilities are. He also placed us in the perfect place in the universe to observe it all. The Earth is perfectly created and situated within our galaxy for observing the universe, not by accident.

The Bible also tells us the history of the human race and how we became separated from God and gradually the relationship became more distant. It also tells us of God's plan for redemption and reconciliation to Himself, but it makes it clear that we also have free will to reject Him and to be eternally separated from Him. That is what this life is all about; the choices we make in this life have eternal consequences.

What are the fruits of a relationship with our Creator? They are joy, comfort, peace, direction, and purpose. He does not give us any assurance of wealth, but He does tell us all of our needs will be met when we trust in Him. We can expect trials and tribulations, all of which have a purpose, and He assures us He will be with us through them all when we put our faith in Him. We are here to be tested, because a faith that is not tested is no faith at all. From this testing, we will grow in character and faith, and be prepared for our role in the Kingdom of God beyond this life. But how did we get separated from God, and how far apart are we?

In Genesis, we find that Adam and Eve walked with their Creator in the Garden of Eden He had prepared for them. Their sin of disobedience caused the Fall of all Creation from the holiness of God. By exercising their free will to disobey what God had told them, Adam and Eve gained knowledge, but with the consequence of living in a cursed environment and eventually, physical death. By the time of Noah, God was so fed up with how evil we had become, he decided to eradicate all of the land animals and humans on the planet except for Noah and his wife, his three sons Shem, Ham and Japheth, and their wives, and pairs of each species of animals for the purpose of starting over after a worldwide flood. God had Noah build an Ark to safely preserve his family and the selected animals during the flood. Many unbelievers scoff at this biblical story, yet every civilization on the planet has a flood story in its history; the geology of the planet is consistent with a worldwide deluge, and geneticists confirm we can all trace our ancestry back to a handful of early humans of every race. Will the discovery of the remains of Noah's Ark convince the skeptics? Probably not, but I believe the day is coming soon when it will be located, thanks to people like Bob Cornuke and the tireless efforts of archeological explorers over the centuries who simply seek the evidence, wherever it may lie. God will reveal it on His timetable.

The Bible then tells us that the common people and common language were confounded in Babylon where they all conspired to build the Tower of Babel and make a name for themselves, again in defiance of God. God caused them to be scattered over the earth and gave them different languages, which is consistent with what we find across the continents today. The Bible gives us detailed lineage from Noah, through ten generations to Abraham. From the time of Abraham and Sarah, we have the history of Israel and the Arab nations and historical collaboration in the Torah, the Bible and the Koran, and the battles of nations were documented. From the early history of Egyptian civilization and the Pharaohs to the Exodus of Israel to Canaan, it is all documented. Bob Cornuke and Larry Williams have explored this in their book "In Search of the Mountain of God." It is also documented in "The Gold of Exodus" (Howard Blum) and "The Exodus Case" (Lennart Mollar).

The new nation of Israel, led out of Egypt by Moses and Aaron, were chosen by God to be His people and given the Law at Mount Sinai. The Law put forth everything God expected for us to be holy and to be able to dwell with Him in heaven. Break any part of the Law, and you have broken the entire Law. It served to demonstrate that no one could keep the Law and to show us our need to be redeemed from our sinful state or be separated from God for eternity. It also pointed the way to the Redeemer and promised His future arrival. From the time of the last prophet in the Old Testament to the birth of Jesus, there are 400 years of silence, no new word from God is documented, but His plan was unfolding in His perfect time.

History and the Bible take us through the rise and fall of the Babylonian Empire in Mesopotamia, The Hittites in Asia Minor, the Assyrian Empire, the Medes and the Persians, the Greek Empire and the Roman Empire during which God sent the promised Messiah to the captive Jews under Roman rulers. This Jesus has had a more profound effect on all of mankind than any other person in human history. He had a dozen or so disciples whom He taught for over three years, and then He was crucified and entombed for three days. On the third day, He was resurrected as prophesied in the Jewish scriptures, and this is attested to by His disciples and hundreds of other witnesses who have documented their accounts in what we call the New Testament today. When Jesus was rejected by His own people as Messiah, He made His offer of redemption available to everyone in the world who would put their faith and trust in Him, and accept the price that He paid for our sins on the cross. This began the Christian faith. Jesus also promised He would be back for His people, and would usher in the Kingdom of God. He will reward the faithful and pronounce the final judgment on those who have rejected Him. His disciples were instructed to spread that "Good News" to every nation. This is our Blessed Hope. The life of Jesus has influenced billions of people; even our modern calendar is based on His birth, now over 2000 years "A.D." – Anno Domini – Latin for "in the year of our Lord", and prior to His birth is referred to as B.C., which stands for "Before Christ". In our politically correct world, most in scholarly circles have recently changed these terms to C. E. for "Common Era" and B.C.E., for "Before the Common Era" so as not to offend other religious and secular sensitivities, but the fact remains that the dividing line of human history is the birth of Jesus Christ, no matter what we call it.

According to Michael Youssef, a period we call "Pre-modernism" began with the collapse of the Roman Empire, in the beginning of the fourth century. People interpreted reality in terms of their knowledge of God. It is characterized by Augustinian thinking and the Word of God.

The "Modern" period began in the early fourteenth century and began the two competing Christian world views of the Reformation and the Renaissance, when the authority of the Roman Catholic Church began replacing the teaching of the Bible. The Renaissance gradually made man displace God as the central focus. The Reformation placed God as Supreme and man was to glorify God. The Renaissance is characterized by "I think, therefore, I am." This was the beginning of secular humanism, where God was dethroned and man was enthroned. It was this thinking that prompted the early pilgrims to seek a land free from this "modern" thinking, and they landed at Plymouth Rock.

By the end of the nineteenth century, man was convinced he could do anything if he put his mind to it, ushering in the "post-modern" era. Truth became relative and meaningless, morality is obsolete. The concept of any ultimate Authority is outmoded, honesty is just for fools. Today this thinking permeates our society, even most of our churches. It has lead to the attitude that Western civilization, dominated by Judeo-Christian thought, is oppressive, and other cultures are superior. Aristotelian logic is out, Eastern mysticism is in. Father God is out, "Mother Earth" is in. Intellect and logic have given way to feelings and opinions. That makes it easy for our society to swallow any kind of lies. There are no rules, just do whatever feels right. Every opinion is equally valid.[d]

History of Belief from AllAboutGOD.com May 02, 2005

Ancient Foundations

The origin of religion can generally be traced to the ancient Near East and classified in three basic categories: polytheistic, pantheistic and monotheistic. Atheism is really a modern belief that resulted from the "Enlightenment" period of the 18th century.

Polytheism

The origin of religion and polytheistic systems: Polytheism (a belief in many gods) is thought to have originated with Hinduism in about 2500 BC. Hindu beliefs were recorded in the Bhagavad Gita, which revealed that many gods were subject to a supreme Brahman god. Polytheism was also the religion of many other ancient cultures, including Assyria, Babylonia, Egypt, Greece and Rome. The ancient polytheistic belief systems viewed gods as being in control of all natural events such as rainfall, harvests and fertility. Generally, polytheistic cultures believed in sacrifices to appease their gods. For instance, the Canaanites sacrificed to the male god, Baal, and his female counterpart, Ashteroth. Baal controlled the rain and the harvest, while Ashteroth controlled fertility and reproduction. The Greeks and Romans developed polytheism to a highly structured pantheon of gods and goddesses.

Pantheism

The origin of religions and pantheistic systems: Pantheism (a belief that all is God) prevailed in numerous ancient cultures. The belief that the universe itself was divine was typified in the Animism beliefs of the African and American Indian cultures, the later Egyptian religion under the Pharaohs, and Buddhism, Confucianism and Taoism in the cultures of the Far East. Pantheistic beliefs are also finding resurgence among various New age movements. Generally, pantheism is the principle that god is everything, and everything is god. Therefore, nature is also part of god. We must be in harmony with nature. We must nurture it and be nurtured by it. Mankind is no different than any other animal. We must live in harmony with them, understand them, and learn from them, focusing on the relationship between mankind and the elements of nature.

Monotheism

The origin of religion and monotheistic systems: Monotheism (a belief in one God) is the foundation of the Judeo-Christian-Muslim line of religions, which began with a man named Abraham in about 2000 BC. From this point in history, God began revealing Himself to the world through the nation of Israel. The Jewish Scriptures record the journey of the Israelites from slaves in Egypt to the "promised land" in Canaan under the leadership of Moses. During a period of about 1500 years, God revealed what became the Old Testament of the Bible, relating the history of Israel with the character and laws of God. During the period of the Roman Empire, Jesus Christ was born in Bethlehem as the long-awaited Messiah. The ministry of Jesus culminated with His crucifixion and resurrection in about 32 AD. After Christ's ascension into heaven, the Christian church grew in His name and the New Testament was written by His disciples. About 600 years later, Muhammad began preaching in Mecca. Muhammad believed he was the ultimate prophet of God, and his teachings became the precepts of Islam as recorded in the Qur'an.

Important Dates in History:

- c. 2000 BC: Time of Abraham, the patriarch of Israel.
- c. 1200 BC: Time of Moses, the Hebrew leader of the Exodus.
- c. 1100 - 500 BC: Hindus compile their holy texts, the Vedas.
- c. 563 - 483 BC: Time of Buddha, founder of Buddhism.
- c. 551 - 479 BC: Time of Confucius, founder of Confucianism.
- c. 200 BC: The Hindu book, Bhagavad Gita, is written.
- c. 2 to 4 BC - 32 AD: Time of Jesus Christ, the Messiah and founder of Christianity.
- c. 32 AD: The Crucifixion and Resurrection of Jesus Christ.
- c. 40 - 90 AD: The New Testament is written by the followers of Jesus Christ.
- c. 570 - 632 AD: Time of Muhammad, who records what later becomes the Qur'an as the basis of Islam.

So this is a brief outline of how we got to where we are today in our religious beliefs, our scientific discoveries, our knowledge of human history and our modern attitudes toward all of these questions of life and our origin. They are documented in the religious texts already mentioned as well as the Jewish sources the Torah, the Mishnah, the Tosefta, and historical documents and the works of secular historians like:

Flavius Josephus – The Works of Josephus (Creation to the
fall of Masada, 73 AD)
Caius Plinius Caecilius Secundus - Letters of the Younger
Pliny (Pliny the Younger)
Cornelius Tacitus – The Annals of Imperial Rome
Eusebius – The History of the Church (Christ to Constantine)
Philo Judaeus of Alexandria – The Works of Philo

Yes, there is a God. Chance did not create the universe or life in it, choice by God did. Chance will determine your eternal destiny (hell) unless you proactively make the right choice. God's fingerprints are all over our universe, we see its Intelligent Design at every level. We have proof in all that is created; we have proof in our written Jewish and Christian history, and a revelation of who He is. The Bible tells us about Him and gives us our purpose. We also have proof from the testimony of reliable witnesses, whose lives were changed by God and who give their lives for that testimony, even today. We have proof in the miracles that were performed during the ministry of Jesus and His Apostles, and we have proof in the accurate fulfillment of hundreds of very specific prophecies that have already come to pass. Only God can foretell the future with 100% accuracy, hundreds or thousands of years before the events occur, and He has done so.

Some of these prophecies have been fulfilled in my lifetime and continue to be fulfilled today, like the regathering of Jews to the Promised Land, their Declaration of Independence and taking the name "Israel" all of which were foretold before the first century AD, but were not fulfilled until 1948 AD. Today there are more than 5 million Jews back in the "Promised Land." The Hebrew language has been revived and is spoken in Israel today. The stumbling block to peace in the Middle East is the disposition of the Temple Mount in Jerusalem, and the division of that city as capital of both the Jews and Palestinians, all of which has been foretold.

Some future prophecies still remain to be fulfilled, promises that God will certainly keep, including the return and revelation of Jesus to the whole world. This generation is witness to it all. The Apostle Paul said, "… if Christ has not been raised, your faith is futile; you are still in your sins… If only for this life we have hope in Christ, we are to be pitied more than all men. (MSG)

Let's look more at our purpose. If God exists and has a purpose for us, why do we have such a hard time with our lives? Why do we suffer hardships and can we avoid them? My son Ben, suffering with strep throat at eight years old asked, "If I never sin again, will I still get sick?" These are great questions we all ask. What are we supposed to do with our life? We'll explore some of these questions in the next chapters.

References and recommended resources:

"**Found: God's Will** – Find the direction and purpose God wants for your life" by John MacArthur Revised © 1977 by SP Publications, Inc..Chariot Victor Publishing, a divsion of Cook Communications, Colorado Springs, Colorado 80918 Grace to You Ministry - ww.gty. org.

"**Why One Way** – Defending an Exclusive Claim in an Inclusive World" by John MacArthur - © 2002 W Publishing Group, A Division of Thomas Nelson Inc., PO Box 141000, Nashville, TN 37216

"**The Battle for the Beginning** – Creation, Evolution and the Bible" by John MacArthur - © 2001 W Publishing Group.

"**The Truth War** – Fighting for Certainty in an Age of Deception" by John MacArthur © 2007 Nelson Books, PO Box 141000, Nashville, TN 37216

"**The Case for Christ**: A Journalist's Personal Investigation of the Evidence for Jesus" by Lee Strobel - © 1998 Zondervan, Grand Rapids, Michigan 49530

"**The Case for Faith**: A Journalist Investigates the Toughest Objections to Christianity" by Lee Strobel – © 2000 Zondervan, Grand Rapids, Michigan 49530

"The Case for a Creator: A Journalist Investigates Scientific Evidence That Points Toward God" by Lee Strobel – © 2004 Zondervan, Grand Rapids, Michigan 49530

"In Six Days - Why Fifty Scientists Choose to Believe in Creation" by John F. Ashton - © 2000 Master Books, Inc. PO Box 727, Green Forest, AR 72638

"The Big Argument: Twenty-Four Scholars Explore How Science, Archaeology, and Philosophy Have Proven the Existence of God" by John F. Ashton & Michael Westacott – © 2005 Master Books, Inc.

"How Christianity Changed the World" by Dr. Alvin J. Schmidt © 2004, Zondervan, Grand Rapids, Michigan 49530

"Darwin on Trial" by Phillip E. Johnson © 1993, InterVarsity Press, PO Box 1400, Downers Grove, IL 60515

"Icons of Evolution – Why much of what we teach about evolution is wrong." By Jonathan Wells © 2000 Regnery Publishing, Inc., One Massachusetts Avenue, NW, Washington, DC 20001

"Darwin's Black Box: The Biochemical Challenge to Evolution" Paperback by Michael J. Behe – © 2006 Free Press, A Division of Simon and Schuster, Inc., Rockefeller Center, 1230 Avenue of the Americas, New York, NY 10020

"A Case against Accident and Self-Organization" by Dean L. Overman © 1997, Rowman & Littlefield Publishers, Inc. 4720 Boston Way, Lanham, Maryland 20706

"I Don't Have Enough Faith to be an Atheist" by Norman L. Geisler and Frank Turek © 2004 by Crossway Books, A division of Good News Publishers, 1300 Crescent St., Wheaton, IL 60187

"God's Plan for the Ages" by Dr. David Reagan © 2005 Lamb & Lion Ministries, P. O. Box 919, McKinney, TX 75070 www.lamblion.com

"The Exodus Case – New Discoveries Confirm the Historical Exodus" by Dr. Lennart Moller © 2002 Scandinavia Publishing House Drejervej 11-21, DK 2400 Copenhagen NV, Denmark

"In Search of the Lost Mountains of Noah" by Robert Cornuke and David Holbrook © 2001 Broadman & Holman Publishers, Nashville, TN www.baseinstitute.org

"In Search of the Lost Mountain of God" by Cornuke & Holbrook © 2000 Broadman & Holman Publishers, Nashville, TN

"Relic Quest" by Robert Cornuke © 2005 Tyndale House Publishers, Inc., Wheaton, IL 60189

"Ark Fever" by Robert Cornuke© 2005 Tyndale House Publishers, Inc., Wheaton, IL 60189

"Jesus Among Other Gods - The Absolute Claims of the Christian Message" by Ravi Zacharias © 2000 W Publishing Group, A Division of Thomas Nelson, Inc., P.O. Box 141000, Nashville, TN 37214 www.rzim.org

"How to Stay Christian in College – An Interactive Guide to Keeping the Faith" by J. Budziszewski © 1999 NavPress, P.O. Box 35001, Colorado Springs, CO 80935

"The Perfect Antidote" sermon by Dr. Michael Youssef www.leadingtheway.org

"The Privileged Planet" video www.equip.org
www.AllAboutGOD.com
http://www.allaboutphilosophy.org/does-god-exist-c.htm

Chapter 2 – Marriage as Intended by God.

R ed Skelton used to joke that marriage is the leading cause of divorce. But for many people, deciding not to marry is not practical, and for someone already married, no longer an option. Too many marriages in the United States end in divorce. The rate is actually beginning to decline after decades of increasing. Part of this decline is due to young people waiting longer to marry while completing education and establishing a career. I belong to a pilot group in which our divorce rate exceeds the national average, which is unconscionably high. Much of this is due to the hardships of living with a traveling spouse and the rigors of temporary single parenting every time the pilot leaves on a trip. Some of it is self-induced when pilots don't honor their marriage commitments. Anyone who travels a lot knows how difficult it is on the whole family; it just doesn't lend itself to the ideal environment for raising children and keeping a strong marital connection. Most in our pilot group are unaware of how rampant this is within our ranks because we keep it secret, we try to compartmentalize our personal problems, or we are embarrassed to admit we need help and seek counseling. We try to fix relationship problems by discarding the relationship; or our spouse does. But that doesn't fix the problem, and we plunge into new relationships hoping for something better, but taking our baggage with us and spreading divorce like disease. What we really need to do is fix the relationship and grow from the experience, emerging healthier, wealthier and wiser. We need to identify what causes the cycle of failed relationships, and how we can break that cycle.

Avoiding divorce requires the cooperation of both the husband and the wife. In all fifty states there is no-fault divorce now. This means that only one party can object to the marriage and file for divorce, and it will be granted, the partner has no legal means to stop the divorce. This has made it so easy to get a divorce that I am convinced it has contributed greatly to the increase in divorce rates since the 1950's in this country, just as legalizing abortions has raised the rate to over a million per month. Many people don't take the marriage vows seriously from the beginning, since we as a society place so little value on marriage; divorce has become easy and commonplace. Maybe it should be more difficult to get married. Even our TV shows make light of marriage with shows like "Desperate Housewives," "Who Wants to Marry a Millionaire?" and "My Big Fat Obnoxious Fiancé." People are marrying for money and entertainment, not giving marriage the respect and sanctity as the sacred institution God intended.

Surprisingly, US News and World Report recently announced the way to find marital bliss is to lower your expectations. I would suggest ensuring your expectations are realistic as one component of a happy, successful marriage. Once you realize that sustained happiness is not something you should expect from marriage, you can be very happy. If you're not happy before marriage, it is not reasonable to expect happiness as a result of marriage. And no one is happy one hundred percent of the time; we all have our ups and downs. In marriage, these emotional cycles require flexibility, patience, listening, understanding, support, empathy and lots of forgiveness.

So how can we realistically stay happily married to one person for a whole lifetime? By keeping our marriage within the boundaries established by the Author of marriage. By keeping the vows that are exchanged in traditional marriage ceremonies. The husband is to love his wife, maintain his sexual integrity, forsaking all others and be a leader in the family. When you are a husband who keeps his word, cherishes his wife, and honors her before friends and family; it makes it easy for your wife to accept your leadership and trust your judgment. He is to receive counsel from his wife and nourish her as the most important person in his world. He must praise her and always value her contributions. The wife is to respect her husband, maintain her sexual integrity and submit to his leadership position in the family. A woman who respects and supports her husband makes it easy for him to honor and appreciate her. Men and women are equal in the eyes of God, but have different roles.

Bob Russell, Senior Minister of Southeast Christian Church in Louisville, KY for over 40 years, and author of numerous books, put it this way: "I know that many people cringe today at the idea of obeying or submitting, but this is not a relationship of servant and master. The reality is leadership is essential in every organization. Business counselors advise against a fifty-fifty partnership because it has such a horrible track record. Someone must have a controlling interest, or the groundwork is laid for division. With leadership comes accountability. God did not leave the leadership of the most important institution He created up to a precarious fifty-fifty partnership. A husband is not to lord over his wife in any way that is demeaning or unloving to her. Biblical submission within marriage is modeled by Jesus and how He was a leader by submitting to the will of the Father. He gave himself up for the sake of those He loves. Husbands are to lead in this unselfish manner as well, sometimes giving up things we desire for the benefit of those we love. What wife would have any difficulty submitting to a husband who has her convinced that he's her slave? Most of the time a husband and wife will be in agreement and live harmoniously, raising the children together, and working toward the same goals in life. When there is a conflict however, if it cannot be resolved by discussion, the wife is to respect the decision of her husband and trust that God will hold him accountable. If your husband is right, you are not embarrassed for insisting on your way. If your husband is wrong, he will suffer the embarrassment and face the consequences for the leadership responsibility he bears. Beth Moore tells wives that submission is you ducking so God can hit your husband."[e]

The Apostle Peter tells us in his first letter that we are to learn from the model Jesus set before us as we grow in Christian maturity. That relationship between Jesus and the Church is how we are to model the marriage between husband and wife. Peter tells wives to love their husbands and respect them and to obey them as the Church is to obey Jesus. In this way, the husband would never ask the wife to sin or suffer abuse, just as Jesus would never ask us to tolerate abuse or to sin. It does mean that the wife should respect her husband and live her life in Christian example, even if her husband is not a Christian. By doing this, many husbands have been won to Christ simply by their actions, without ever saying a word.

One of the most famous examples of this today is that of Lee Strobel who was a committed atheist until his wife became a Christian. As he saw the changes in her life, he began to feel convicted and curious. As an investigative reporter with a legal background, he set out to prove that Jesus and the Bible were a big scam, and put his professional skills to work to debunk the whole thing (as many have tried before him). As a result, he is now a Christian minister, and the author of many books *confirming* the truth of the Bible and the reality of Jesus being who He claims to be, the evidence is overwhelming. All because his wife did what the Bible said she should do. A proper Christian marriage is a loving, respectful, joyous relationship!

Peter goes on to tell us that husbands are supposed to live with their wives in an understanding way and to honor them as the weaker vessel, since they also are heirs of God's grace of life, and so *that his prayers may not be hindered.* When a man is not living up to his role in the marriage, God will not hear his prayers until he repents and heals the relationship with his wife and with God. When Peter speaks of the "weaker vessel," he likely has several things in mind. First, in general, most men are physically stronger than women and could use their strength against their wives. Second, in Peter's day women were considered weaker in dignity than men, even considered as property. Unfortunately, we can see an implicit assumption of this in our own society today in our overt objectification of women in every form of media and pornography. We are no better today than they were in Peter's day in many ways. Third, Peter may also be speaking of women having lesser authority in the marriage relationship. So Peter calls on husbands to treat wives with honor, dignity and respect and exercise their leadership with love and consideration. *When this is done, their prayers are not hindered.*

Paul confirms this in Ephesians 5, and Jesus gave several parable examples of this type of relationship.

If the wife does not fulfill her responsibility in the family, she makes it nearly impossible for the husband to fulfill his leadership role. He needs her to be a helper, to support and encourage him. Sometimes she needs to intercede on his behalf and pray for him.

Let me reiterate: Biblical submission does NOT mean any woman should tolerate any kind of abuse of herself or her children. Physical safety must always come first. Nor should husbands allow abuse to occur in the family. If you are in a situation that is abusive, find a safe place first, and then deal with the relationship issues after the abuse is dealt with.

I see many in our pilot group who do not honor their spouse or their marriage. They have few kind words to say about their spouse, or live separate lives to avoid conflict. On layovers, some are met by girlfriends or head to the nude bars. They take off their wedding rings, or just never wear them at all. Your marriage does not end at 3000' within a fifty mile range of your hometown airport. When returning home from a weeklong trip, I see some of our pilots head to the golf course with their buddies the next day, when they should be spending time with their spouse and reconnecting in the relationship. Just being roommates isn't honoring the marriage. Any modification to marriage that is not a part of the original design weakens the marriage and the original design is one man and one woman for one lifetime together. Act as if your spouse were with you at all times, because they should be, in your heart and on your mind. Be a parent your children can be proud of, by modeling the kind of marriage you would want for them. Why be married if you don't want the kind of role described in the Bible? That IS what marriage is! That is how God created it to be. Anything else is just "playing house" and will not succeed as a marriage, because it is not marriage. This behavior is certainly not unique to pilots.

In the book, "His Needs, Her Needs", Willard Harley accurately points out that the needs of the man and wife are different, but should be complementary. A woman typically needs affection, conversation, trust, financial security, and family commitment. A man needs sexual fulfillment, a recreational companion, an attractive spouse, domestic support, and admiration. Ideally, when she gets what she wants, he gets what he wants, (usually in that order).

In another book, "Every Man's Marriage", Stephen Arterburn offers these love chillers:

Men are rebellious by nature, more so than women, as evidenced by our far greater crime rates.

The male ego is bigger, but more fragile than the female ego. This fragility usurps intimacy with our wives. This is why men don't like to show emotions for fear of vulnerability to being hurt. This also causes us to see our wife's superior gifts as a threat to our ego.

Men are relatively less sensitive to the needs of others.

Men are less able to express emotions and feelings *verbally* than women are.

The male brain is more oriented to facts and logic than to emotions and intuitions. We are literally wired differently!

Men are sexually stimulated visually. This means we are more tempted to stray sexually than women are. Rather than taking responsibility for what we allow our eyes to view, we blame it on God for making us that way. This visual roaming disconnects you from your wife.

Before marriage, males take responsibility for nurturing the love relationship. This must not stop after marriage, but it usually does.

Men need less romance than women. You see your wife naked, and you're ready to slide in bed with her. She still wants and needs to be romanced with your time, attention, memories and dreams together.

The male shield from inferiority is his work. Your wife's shield from inferiority is you, so she naturally places a higher value on the marital relationship than you do.

Men desire peace from marriage, while women desire oneness.

No one person is going to meet all of your needs, and they shouldn't be expected to. While your spouse should be the focal point and priority of your adult relationships, s/he should not be the only source of all that you need. Your sexual satisfaction must be an exclusive relationship with your spouse, but you both should have some same-sex friends or other couples for recreation, entertainment or hobbies, conversation and support. Sometimes you need to have a same-sex friend or family member you can consult when you have a disagreement with your spouse, someone you respect and trust to give good advice and hold you accountable to your spouse. Someone who is always on your side, even when you disagree. This might be an accountability partner from a small group Bible study.

Love is an action, a verb! Love is not just an emotion you feel. Feelings are the product of action. Love is not self-gratification; that is selfishness! Love is something we do, not what we feel. Love is a choice! It's taking care of someone in need. It's sacrificing our wants to put someone else before us. Make others feel important. Make the relationship more valuable than your rights. Ladies, men can NOT read minds! You must talk to him in a language he understands to get your needs met. *And probably more than once.*

Resolving conflicts - here, communication truly is the key. Couples who do not talk and listen to each other when they disagree are destined for disappointment. One difficulty unique to traveling husbands is the transfer of power as the husband comes and goes. Obviously, when the husband leaves on a trip, the wife is left to run the household and keep up all of the daily chores, some of which might be done by the husband when he is home, but falls to the wife or children in his absence. This usually is not a problem, but what about the occasional emergency? The car won't start, a water pipe froze, the builder got the wrong bathtub, your pregnant wife's water broke, hopefully, not all of these at once. You need to have a plan for these kinds of contingencies when you are out of touch with your family. Have a handyman or a list of reputable contractors that can take immediate action when needed. Join the American Automobile Association or another roadside assistance service. Get support through your church, from friends, neighbors and nearby family members. Then, stay in touch as much as possible on the road, to stay in the loop when things do need attention.

It is important to discuss parenting issues and agree on daily standards for behavior and exposure to age-appropriate entertainment. Having both parents in agreement on these issues before they arise can avoid many conflicts and keep the home spouse comfortable in the knowledge that they are doing things right; they will feel more supported. It also removes the ability of children to divide and conquer when the parents are of one mind.

31

How can we repair an unstable marriage? Start by staying in it. Resolve to fix it. Quitting (divorce) is not an option, at least as much as it depends on you. Talk about the things that bother you before they accumulate the mass of a black hole. You won't always agree, but you can always find a compromise, and you can always choose to love and respect your spouse. Men, love your wife even when she doesn't deserve it. Wives, respect your husband, even when he doesn't deserve it. God loves us, even when we are unlovable, even though we are rebellious and ungrateful. Offer forgiveness and re-commit to doing it right. Do the next right thing. Get counseling when you can't resolve a conflict. Pick your battles carefully. Not every skirmish requires a nuclear response. Divorce is a weapon of mass destruction.

If you have to have the last word in an argument, make sure it's an apology. The goal is not to win the argument; the goal is to resolve the conflict. Be anxious to forgive.

These twelve words from Bob Russell may be the most important to remember:

I was wrong
I am sorry
Please forgive me
I love you

Find ways of continually expressing love. "The Five Love Languages" by Gary Chapman expresses the five most common ways people show their appreciation and affection. One or more of these will likely suit your spouse:

Gift giving
Physical touch
Acts of service
Words of affirmation
Quality (meaningful) time together

Communicating thoughts and feelings seems to come much easier for most women than it does for men. Many troubled marriages cite

32

communication problems as the number one factor. Most men don't naturally communicate their feelings for fear of exposure. Some don't want anyone to see any side of them that may not be very manly, like things they are afraid of, or embarrassing things like crying or showing any signs of weakness. We are afraid that if these "faults" are exposed, we aren't very masculine, or we might not be accepted as we are. Some of us may have some real faults that we need to work on but don't want to face, like addiction to pornography or other private behaviors. Exposing these would make us accountable to someone else who might force us to work on these areas and develop some real character. If you can't do this with your wife, get with a group of men who will help you become accountable and who understand the struggle, men who have been there and overcome that. We become men in the presence of men, not by conquering women.

The dichotomy in all of this is that we get in trouble when we are not communicating and not sharing our whole self with our spouse, afraid of becoming vulnerable. Yet we are afraid of sharing because we might get in trouble. The fact is, exposing your whole self to your spouse does not *create* problems, it *prevents* them. Only by exposing our weaknesses can we overcome them, turn them into strengths and strengthen our relationship.

For those who have good marriages but simply hate the temporary separation from a traveling spouse, I recommend the book "Keeping Your Family Close When Frequent Travel Pulls You Apart" by Elizabeth Hoekstra. First printed in 1998, it gives some imaginative ideas for staying connected when physically separated. There are some humorous and heart-wrenching glimpses of real-life situations that offer help and hope to those of us who travel frequently. She only briefly mentions the use of a beeper or computer for email to help stay in touch. Today, more travelers have laptops with wireless access or PDA's that would allow you to extrapolate her suggestions to using these electronic devices to store or send family photos, or some home movie or sound clips, emails and cell phone calls to stay connected to family and be a part of home decision-making and events in real time, or nearly so. Today it's easier than ever before to stay connected, there's no excuse not to.

God intended your marriage to be fulfilling for a lifetime. Most of us did not have perfect parents who modeled a perfect marriage. That is why God provided the biblical model of marriage, so we can all see what He intended marriage to be. Over and over He uses a marriage illustration to demonstrate His love for us and His commitment to us in the Bible. That is the model He wants us to emulate and pass on to our children, a model that teaches them and gives them security and maturity. If your marriage never matures because someone bails when the going gets tough, you'll never see how good it can be on the other side of the tribulation. You can emerge stronger and more deeply committed than if you quit.

For more information:

Books:
"How We Love – A Revolutionary Approach to Deeper Connections in Marriage" by Milan & Kay Yerkovich © 2006, Waterbrook Press, A division of Random House Inc., 12265 Oracle Blvd., Suite 200, Colorado Springs, CO 80921 (Get the workbook also!)

"Love and Respect – The Love She Most Desires, The Respect He Desperately Needs." by Dr. Emerson Eggerichs © 2004 Integrity Publishers, 5250 Virginia Way, Suite 110, Brentwood, TN 37027

"Boundaries in Marriage - When to say yes, when to say no." by Drs. Henry Cloud and John Townsend © 1999 Zondervan Publishing House, Grand Rapids, MI 49530

"Safe People - How to find relationships that are good for you and avoid those that aren't" by Drs. Henry Cloud and John Townsend © 1995 Zondervan Publishing House, Grand Rapids, MI 49530

"Boundaries Face to Face – How to have that difficult conversation you've been avoiding" by Drs. Henry Cloud and John Townsend © 2003 Zondervan Publishing House, Grand Rapids, MI 49530

"His Needs, Her Needs – Building An Affair-proof Marriage" by Willard F. Harley, Jr. © 1986, 1994 Fleming H. Revell, a division of Baker Book House Company, P.O. Box 6287, Grand Rapids, MI 49516

"Every Woman's Marriage - Igniting the joy & passion you both desire" by Shannon & Greg Ethridge © 2006 Waterbrook Press,

A division of Random House Inc., 12265 Oracle Blvd., Suite 200, Colorado Springs, CO 80921

"Every Man's Marriage – Every Man's Guide to... Winning the Heart of a Woman"* by Steven Arterburn, Fred Stoeker & Mike Yorkey © 2001 Waterbrook Press, A division of Random House Inc., 2375 Telstar Drive, Suite 160, Colorado Springs, CO 80920 *"Every Woman's Desire" has been retitled and released as "Every Man's Marriage"

"The Five Love Languages – How to Express Heartfelt Commitment to Your Mate" by Gary Chapman © 1992, 1995 Northfield Publishing, 215 West Locust St., Chicago, IL 60610

"Love, Sex and Lasting Relationships – God's Prescription for Enhancing Your Love Life" by Chip Ingram © 2003 Baker Books, a division of Baker Book House Company, P.O. Box 6287, Grand Rapids, MI 49516

"Husbands Who Won't Lead & Wives Who Won't Follow – Help in understanding your mate, your marriage and your expectations for each other" by James Walker © 1989 Bethany House Publishers, 11400 Hampshire Ave. South, Bloomington, MN 55438

"Keeping Your Family Close When Frequent Travel Pulls You Apart" by Elizabeth M. Hoekstra, © 1998 Crossway Books, a division of Good News Publishers, 1300 Crescent St., Wheaton, IL 60187

Audio:
    "Essentials for a Happy Marriage" Bob Russell sermon series www.livingword.org.

Websites:

www.cloudtownsend.com	Drs. Henry Cloud and John Townsend resources
www.promisekeepers.org	Promise Keepers - For men. Support groups, local contacts
www.newlife.com	New Life Live - For everyone. Free tips and incredible resources
www.southeastchristian.org	Church in SDF Support groups, counseling, media center, bookstore

www.livingword.org	SECC media ministry Resources for www. everyone
www.family.org	Focus on the Family Resources for everyone.
www.troubledwith.com	Focus on the Family Resources for everyone
www.fltoday.org	Family Life Today Resources for everyone

Phone numbers:

    1-800 New Life   24 hour helpline and crisis intervention

Chapter 3 – Children

Raising children has always been real work, if it is done right. Too many children are raising themselves or being raised by television because parents are too busy for them. God never intended for us to turn our kids over to the public schools for education, and the children's ministry at church for their spiritual foundations. These must be overseen and supplemented by the parents. It is the parents who will be held accountable by God for what their children are exposed to and taught, or what has been omitted from their education. Just as God has a purpose for marriage, it is the foundation of the family:

NLT Malachi 2:15 Didn't the LORD make you one with your wife? In body and spirit you are His. And what does He want? **Godly children from your union**. So guard yourself; remain loyal to the wife of your youth.

NIV Deu 11:18 Fix these words of mine in your hearts and minds; tie them as symbols on your hands and bind them on your foreheads. **Teach them to your children**, talking about them when you sit at home and when you walk along the road, when you lie down and when you get up.

If you don't have plans for your children, the world does. And the world's plan for them is not God's plan for them. Parents MUST be proactive in both teaching and shielding their children. Christians must live in this world for now, but remember, and pass on to our children that we are not OF this world! Ultimately, our home is in the kingdom of God!

NLT Romans 12:2 Don't copy the behavior and customs of this world, but let God transform you into a new person by changing the way you think. Then you will know what God wants you to do, and you will know how good and pleasing and perfect his will really is.

NIV Mark 10:14 When Jesus saw this, he was indignant. He said to them, "Let the little children come to me, and do not hinder them, for the kingdom of God belongs to such as these.

NIV Mark 10:15 I tell you the truth, anyone who will not receive the kingdom of God like a little child will never enter it."

George Barna points out that children matter to God and they are very precious to Him. We need to see them the same way:

> *Children are a gift from God.* He grants children to adults as a special sign of His love to us and as a means of personal fulfillment. (Deut. 7:13; Ps. 127:3).
>
> *Adults receive special blessings through their children.* God provides supernatural benefits of many types to family and friends through children, and He matures us through the challenges of parenting. (Num. 5:28; Deut. 28:4, 11; Lam. 4:2).
>
> *Children are desirable.* From the beginning of human history, God has instructed us to have children. In fact, the intentional decision of a married couple not to have children is viewed as a bad choice. (Gen 9:7, Deut. 6:3, Luke 1:24, 25).
>
> *Children need to be taught how to think and act in relation to God and His ways.* One of the greatest adult challenges is passing on appropriate knowledge and behaviors to their progeny. We were created to be in relationship with Him, so our understanding of His nature and expectations is a significant undertaking. (Exod. 12:26, 37; Deut. 4:9, 10; 6:1-7; 31:12, 13; Ps.78:4-6; Prov. 22:6).
>
> *To have a fruitful relationship with God, children must be taught to obey Him.* Obedience is one of the central duties of humankind. Throughout scripture, God exhorts his people

to be raised to follow His commands and reap the benefits of such obedience. (Prov. 8:32; 19:26; Jer. 2:30; 3:22; Eph. 6:1; Col. 3:20).

Children are so valuable to God that He commands us to protect them. Parents are supposed to ensure the spiritual and physical security of their children. (1 Sam. 20:42; Ezra 8:21).

God wants to have a genuine relationship with His children. Accordingly, He describes how children may enter His presence and enjoy His company. (Ps. 8:2; 34:11; 103:13; Mal. 2:15; Matt. 21:15; Mark 10:13-16).

God loves children enough to ensure they receive discipline. Regardless of the manner in which that shaping is provided, it is a reflection of His passion for a child's well-being. (Prov. 3:11-12; 13:24; 19:18; 23:13; 29:15-17; Eph. 6:4).

God enjoys the nature and personality of children. The Scriptures specifically identify attributes such as sincerity, humility, naiveté, vulnerability and simplicity as qualities found in children, and He treasures these characteristics. (Matt. 18:3; 19:14; Phil. 2:15).[f]

Raising children is best accomplished when they have both parents living with them daily. That is the ideal that God intended for the best outcome. The Bible is full of illustrations of how NOT to raise children, and we are to learn from these lessons. I have heard many people say that kids don't come with an instruction manual. While that is true, that doesn't mean the manual doesn't exist. There have been many written, find one that is based on a sound understanding of Scripture. Some are listed at the end of this chapter, and they will be much more comprehensive than what I intend for this chapter. I'll just be highlighting some tips here that I think are most helpful in parenting. You'll find more in chapter twelve.

We are inundated with daily news of kidnappings. We see the faces of missing and exploited children on milk cartons and mailings. Now we have a nationwide Amber Alert system to quickly notify communities or the whole country of missing people when foul play is suspected. We live in perilous times, and all of this underscores the need to watch our children closely and be involved in their lives and supervise what they are exposed to.

The most difficult thing to provide our kids with these days is our time. But we MUST make time for them until they are self-sufficient, Godly adults and our training them is complete. Then they will be able to train their own children from their experience and parental modeling. What do we teach them? John MacArthur lists these Proverbs:

1. To have a healthy fear of (reverence for) God (1:7; 9:10; 10:27; 14:26-27; 15:16; 16:6; 19:23)
2. To guard their minds (4:23; 23:7)
3. To obey you (1:8; 4:1-4; 6:20-23; 30:17)
4. To carefully select their companions (1:11-18; 2:10-15; 13:20)
5. To control their sinful desires (2:16-19; 5:3-5; 6:23-33; 7:6-27)
6. To enjoy sexual fidelity in marriage (5:15-20)
7. To watch their words (4:24; 10:11, 19-21, 32; 12:18, 22; 15:1-2, 7; 16:23; 20:15)
8. To pursue their work (6:6-11; 10:4-5; 22:29)
9. To manage their money (3:9-10; 11:24-26; 19:17; 22:9)
10. To love their neighbors (3:27-29; 25:21-22)[g]

Here are some ways we can improve as Dads:

10 Do's and don'ts for Dads from New Life Ministries

1. Connect before you correct. Part of every Dad's role is to bring a healthy sense of structure and discipline to the family. Communicating with your child, which includes listening to their "side" of the issue, is a key first step in successful, loving discipline.
2. Be there. One of the great myths is that a little "quality" time makes up for a substantial "quantity" of time. Going to school, sporting and other events is a big deal! It says - "I have your

best interests at the center of my heart" to your child. *Don't think only about your own affairs, but be interested in others and what they are doing.* ~ Philippians 2:4

3. Express love often. Kids (especially pre-teens and teens) act like they don't want their parents to "make a fuss" over them. It's just an act. Kids need hugs and kisses ... affirm them at every opportunity.

4. Phony, macho men are only heroes in the movies. Real Dads aren't perfect. You can be a hero to your children if you open your heart to them and admit when you've made mistakes. They have an enormous capacity to forgive and their hearts' desire is to love and be loved. *People who cover over their sins will not prosper. But if they confess and forsake them, they will receive mercy.* ~ Proverbs 28:13

5. Never make your child choose between parents. If you have problems with your wife, don't try to convince your child that you're "right" or the "victim". This causes an emotional split in your child and will ultimately drive him or her further away from you. Confine the adult issues to the adults.

6. Love your wife. The greatest Dad in the world will minimize the true impact he has on his children if he does not model Godly intimacy in front of his kids. That's where the cornerstone of their future marriage is laid. *Since God chose you to be the holy people whom He loves, you must clothe yourselves with tenderhearted mercy, kindness, humility, gentleness, and patience. You must make allowance for each other's faults and forgive the person who offends you ... And the most important piece of clothing you must wear is love. Love is what binds us all together in perfect harmony.* ~ Colossians 3:12-14

7. Be consistent. When you are consistent in your actions, love and discipline, an environment of safety and security is created. Kids need to know that there are some things they can always count on. *Discipline your child while there is hope. If you don't, you will ruin their lives.* ~ Proverbs 19:18

8. Be careful, you're in the spotlight. Your kids are watching every move you make. To some extent, their picture of you shapes their picture of their Heavenly Father. You have the opportunity

to create a positive, loving image or a confusing and untrust-worthy one. Instead, there must be a spiritual renewal of your thoughts and attitudes. *You must display a new nature because you are a new person, created in God's likeness - righteous, holy and true.* ~ Ephesians 4:23,24

9. Guard your tongue. The words you speak to your children can cut like a knife or send them soaring like a rocket. They will remember some things you say in passing for the rest of their lives. *Kind words are like honey - sweet to the soul and healthy for the body.* ~ Proverbs 16:24

10. Develop Godly character. Nothing will influence your children more than watching you grow in your relationship with God. You can preach the Gospel by your actions much more effectively than you can by your words. *And now, just as you accepted Christ Jesus as your Lord, you must continue to live in obedience to Him. Let your roots grow down into Him and draw up nourishment from Him, so you will grow in faith, strong and vigorous in the truth you were taught. Let your lives overflow with thanksgiving for all He has done.* ~ Colossians 2:6,7 [h]

Here are some creative ways to connect with your kids from the book "Parents Guide to Top 10 Dangers Teens Face" (from New Life Ministries):

1. Break through superficial conversations by asking probing questions like, "What's going well in your life? What's not going well? What changes would you like to make? What's the biggest challenge you're currently facing?"

2. Ask your child to pick a new sport, hobby, art project, or interest for the two of you to develop together.

3. Take your child out to breakfast with no agenda-and just listen.

4. Visit a rest home together, and discuss feelings about death, dying, and aging.

5. Keep a journal of family highlights and special accomplishments throughout the year and review it together on December 31st.

6. Tell your children one of your fears, and do something together that challenges your fear. If you fear flying, fly. If you fear water, swim.

7. Write your child a letter, saying what you enjoy in your life, what you don't, how you have succeeded, where you made mistakes, and what you hope he or she can learn from your life.

8. Research the meaning of your child's name and point out the character traits that parallel the name. Explain why you chose that name.

9. Discover your child's favorite song. Then, listen to it, go over the words, discuss what they mean, and ask what makes the song a favorite.

10. Select a classic from literature, and have a family reading time at least once a week.

11. Ask your child three places he or she would like to visit within driving distance, and make a plan to see them during the next year.

12. Record your family tree as far back as possible. List one or two prominent character traits associated with each family member. See if you can identify patterns that run through your family.

13. Play board games or cards with your child, and use the time to find out what's going on in his or her life.

14. Read, watch or listen to "Every Young Man's Battle" with your son and talk about it. For daughters, read "Every Young Woman's Battle."

15. Adopt a grandparent in a nursing home.[i]

If we are doing all of these things, then we will know our children well, and they will know us. We must safeguard what they see on television, in our homes and out. We must keep them safe on the internet with the use of filters and supervision. Computers should be in open areas of the home where anyone passing by will be able to monitor what is being accessed to ensure it is appropriate. We need to know who our young kids are corresponding with in emails and chat rooms, and never allow them to meet someone without our supervision. We need to know what the curricula are in our schools, what kids are taught and that it fits the Christian world view.

Stepfamilies present unique circumstances that the traditional family does not normally have to deal with. There are step family resources listed at the end of this chapter that may be very helpful as well the other resources listed. Here are "Ten Keys to a Healthy Step Family" from New Life Ministries:

1. **You must "connect" with the children at their point of emotional need.** Remarriage is a challenge for everyone, but especially the children. For most children, their parent's decision to remarry represents the loss of the dream that their biological parents will reunite. Even children whose parents had a terrible relationship have the fantasy that someday everyone will be happy. The grief associated with this loss is painful and can last a long time.
2. **Encourage your children to talk about their feelings.** You may not like everything you hear, but your children need a safe and nurturing environment to respectfully share their emotions. The best way to encourage your children to open up is to set the example. When you are transparent about your feelings you foster the security and trust they long for.
3. **Have realistic expectations.** Getting to know each other will take time. You will not experience instant intimacy, trust and respect. The expectation of quickly becoming "one big happy family" will set you up for disappointment every time. *Hope deferred makes the heart sick...* Prov. 13:12.
4. **Establish new family traditions and rituals.** Every family needs to develop its own culture. By establishing traditions and rituals for your new family you provide a greater sense of belonging for everyone involved. Including the children in the process will increase their level of support and cooperation.
5. **Be sensitive to traditions that have already been established in your child's life, even if they don't include you.** If your child has always visited their grandparents for a week during the summer or spent Christmas Eve with their non-custodial parent, don't suddenly change those traditions. The resentment your child may feel could undermine all your efforts to create new, positive memories.

6. **Don't trash your child's other biological parent.** By showing respect and civility to the other biological parent you minimize conflict and actually strengthen your relationship with your children. As bad as some situations can get, control your feelings and comments. *So then, let us pursue the things which make for peace and the building up of one another.* Romans 14:19.

7. **The marriage relationship must be a priority.** Every successful blended family has one common characteristic - a strong bond between the husband and wife. Couples in blended families have incredible distractions in their lives compared to most first marriages. Ex-spouses, in-laws, financial obligations, new schools and new homes can rock the foundation of the marriage.

8. **Parents must clearly define and consistently follow through with rules for discipline.** Many stepparents tend to be too lenient with their new stepchildren in hopes of winning their acceptance and approval. This approach never works. All children need and expect to have boundaries in place, and consistent discipline is one of the most effective and powerful ways of communicating love and respect.

9. **Both parents must be involved in establishing the rules for discipline.** Parents must always present a unified front when enforcing the rules. Children are very smart and will try to figure out how to play their parents against one another. Parents who don't allow their unity to be broken are much more likely to gain respect and obedience from their children.

10. **Place God in the center of your home.** The ultimate key to every family's success, no matter what the circumstances are, is choosing to make God the centerpiece of your home. To be the kind of parent or spouse you want to be requires wisdom, patience and love. The best way for you to develop these character traits is to have a vibrant relationship with God. *But seek first His kingdom and His righteousness and all these things shall be added to you.* Matt. 6:33

According to Chip Ingram, all kids basically need two things from parents. They need to know they are significant, and they need to know they are safe. They constantly want the answers to these two questions: Do you love me and where are the boundaries? Give them those assurances and you are off to a good start. Stepparents have additional challenges to get all parents, stepparents, grandparents and caregivers on board, so they must choose wisely and work hard to see that all of these people who influence their children are working together toward the same goal: raising Godly children!

Parenting: What is the goal of your parenting?

Survival – keep things on an even keel day to day.
Independence – teach children to be self-sufficient.
Competence – teach children to be capable.
Problem solving – address problems as they arise.
Morality – teach children to be good.
Religious life – teach children to have God at the center of their lives.

The Real Goal

Good kids are a product of the real goal of parenting: *mature character*. When children grow up with mature character, they are able to take their place as adults in the world and function properly in all areas of life. Character growth is the main goal of child rearing.

But what is character? For some, the word character brings to mind pictures of a person who has integrity, takes responsibility for her life, and stands up for the right thing. Others may see character as the child's personality—those attributes that make her unique, such as energy level, interests, and a sense of humor.

People with mature character do have traits of integrity, responsibility and courage, but we understand character in a bigger-picture way. We view character as the structures and abilities within ourselves that make up how we operate in life. In other words, character is the sum of our abilities to deal with life as God designed us to. Reality makes certain demands on us, for example, to relate to other people in good ways, to do what we say we will do, to take ownership of our own mistakes, and to solve our own problems.

Our success (or failure) in meeting these demands shows our level of character development.

You may know adults who look good and perform well but have character flaws. These character flaws—a bad temper, a tendency to withdraw, or self-centeredness—rear their ugly heads over and over again to diminish that person's life experience. More often than not, these flaws began in childhood and continued on in adulthood. This is why parenting is so critical; childhood is the time when character strengths and weaknesses are laid down. This is not to scare you, but simply to point out the truth. You can make great strides in helping your child be a person of character, or you can also miss its importance and see its effects in painful ways later in life.[j]

Resources:

"Transforming Children into Spiritual Champions – Why Children Should Be Your Church's #1 Priority" by George Barna © 2003 Regal Books/Gospel Light P.O.Box 3875, Ventura, CA 93006

"Complete Book of Baby and Child Care" by Focus on the Family Physicians Resource Council © 1997 Tyndale House Publishers, Wheaton, IL 60189

"The Complete Parenting Book" by Drs. David and Jan Stoop © 2004 Fleming H. Revell, a division of Baker Publishing Group, P.O. Box 6287, Grand Rapids, MI 49516

"Helping the Struggling Adolescent – A Guide to Thirty-Six Common Problems for Counselors, Pastors, and Youth Workers" by Dr. Les Parrott III © 1993, 2000 Zondervan, Grand Rapids, MI 49530

"The Most Important Place on Earth – What A Christian Home Looks Like and How to Build One" by Robert Wolgemuth © 2004 Nelson Books, Nashville, TN

"Successful Christian Parenting – Raising Your Child With Care, Compassion, and Common Sense" by John MacArthur © 1998 Word Publishing, A Thomas Nelson Company, Nashville, TN

"Raising Great Kids – A Comprehensive Guide to Parenting with Grace and Truth" by Drs. Henry Cloud and John Townsend © 1999 Zondervan Publishing House, Grand Rapids, MI 49530

"Boundaries with Kids – When to Say Yes, When to Say No to Help Your Children Gain Control of Their Lives" by Drs. Henry Cloud and John Townsend © 1998 Zondervan Publishing House, Grand Rapids, MI 49530

"Boundaries with Teens – When to Say Yes, How to Say No" by Dr. John Townsend © 2006 Zondervan Publishing House, Grand Rapids, MI 49530

"You Can't Make Me! – But I Can Be Persuaded" Strategies for bringing out the best in your strong-willed child, by Cynthia Ulrich Tobias © 1999 Waterbrook Press, A division of Random House Inc., 2375 Telstar Drive, Suite 160, Colorado Springs, CO 80920

"The New Strong-Willed Child – Birth Through Adolescence" by Dr. James Dobson © 1978, 2004 Tyndale House Publishers, Wheaton, IL 60189

"The New Dare to Discipline" by Dr. James Dobson © 1970, 1992 Tyndale House Publishers, Wheaton, IL 60189

"Bringing up Boys – Practical advice and encouragement for those shaping the next generation of men" by Dr. James Dobson © 2001 Tyndale House Publishers, Wheaton, IL 60189

"How a Man Prepares His Daughters for Life" by Michael Farris © 1996 Bethany House Publishers, 11400 Hampshire Ave. South, Bloomington, MN 55438

"How to Stay Christian in College – An Interactive Guide to Keeping the Faith" by J. Budziszewski © 1999 NavPress, P.O. Box 35001, Colorado Springs, CO 80935

"How to Stay Christian in High School" by Steve Gerali © 2004 TH1NK, NavPress, P.O. Box 35001, Colorado Springs, CO 80935

"Preparing Your Son for Every Man's Battle – Honest Conversations About Sexual Integrity" by Stephen Arterburn, Fred Stoeker, Mike Yorkey © 2003 Waterbrook Press., 2375 Telstar Drive, Suite 160, Colorado Springs, CO 80920

"Preparing Your Daughter for Every Woman's Battle – Creative Conversations about Sexual and Emotional Integrity" by Shannon Ethridge © 2005 Waterbrook Press, 2375 Telstar Drive, Suite 160, Colorado Springs, CO 80920

"What a Difference a Daddy Makes – The Indelible Imprint a Dad Leaves on His Daughter's Life" by Dr. Kevin Leman © 2000 Thomas Nelson Books, Nashville, TN
"Raising Great Kids" seminars   www.cloudtownsend.com
www.newlife.com   1-800-NEWLIFE 24 hour helpline
www.family.org   Focus on the Family website
www.troubledwith.com   Focus on the Family helpsite
www.thetotaltransformation.com   James Lehman on parenting
www.escapeschool.com   Abduction prevention program

Step-Family Resources:
"The Smart Step-Family – Seven Steps to a Healthy Family" by Ron L. Deal © 2002 Bethany House Publishers, 11400 Hampshire Ave. South, Bloomington, MN 55438
"The Blended Family" by Tom and Adrienne Frydenger © 1984 Chosen Books, a division of Baker Book House, P.O. Box 6287, Grand Rapids, MI 49516
"Stepfamily Problems – How to Solve Them" by Tom and Adrienne Frydenger © 1991 Fleming H. Revell, a division of Baker Book House, P.O. Box 6287, Grand Rapids, MI 49516
"Living in a Step-Family Without Getting Stepped On – Helping Your Children Survive the Birth Order Blender" by Dr. Kevin Leman © 1994 Thomas Nelson Books, Nashville, TN

www.realfamilies.com   Resources from Dr. Kevin Leman
www.successfulstepfamilies.com   Resources from Ron L. Deal
www.familylife.com Resources from Dennis and Barbara Rainey
www.fltoday.org   Family Life Today ministry with Dennis
       Rainey

   "How to Raise Positive Kids in a Negative World" sermon series by Chip Ingram

"Single Parenting that Works!" Video Seminar Speaker: Dr. Kevin Leman www.realfamilies.com
"Bringing Peace and Harmony to the Blended Family" Video Seminar Speaker: Dr. Kevin Leman www.realfamilies.com

Section Two – Challenges to Life: "You will have trials and tribulation…"

Chapter 4 – Facing Divorce

"I don't love you anymore." "My feelings for you are gone." It often starts like that, or worse, by the revelation of an inappropriate extramarital relationship. Maybe it's just silence. How did it get like this? Is the marriage salvageable? The answer to the second question depends largely on the answer to the first. Every person seeking counsel is looking for one thing: Hope. We all want assurance that there is life after a bad relationship, or that the relationship can be redeemed, hope for ourselves and our children.

Marriage is designed to bring a man and woman together to become one with each other. It is beautiful when done right, misery if neglected or abused. Becoming one with your spouse means dying to self and putting the other person first. Every unhappy marriage has one thing in common: someone is not getting what they want; their expectations are not being met. So, to ensure the greatest likelihood for success in marriage we need to have realistic expectations and ensure that these expectations are met for both the husband and wife.

This description of love is commonly read at traditional weddings: NIV 1 Corinthians 13:4-8 Love is patient, love is kind. It does not envy, it does not boast, it is not proud. It is not rude, it is not self-seeking, it is not easily angered, it keeps no record of wrongs. Love does not delight in evil but rejoices with the truth. It always protects, always trusts, always hopes, always perseveres. Love never fails.

These are all verbs, action words, not feelings, because that's what love is, it is an action, not a feeling that comes and goes. It is keeping a commitment. None of us would divorce our children because we don't love them anymore; we have a commitment to raise them to be self-sufficient, responsible adults. So, what happens after the wedding ceremony to cause someone to divorce their spouse after that lifetime commitment to love, share and care for that person (which exceeds the commitment to your children!)? Are we taking these vows too lightly? I think so. However, staying married is not just up to you. A lasting marriage requires the cooperation and continued commitment of both people. Today, with "no-fault" divorce laws, any person can easily divorce their spouse without their consent by simply claiming "irreconcilable differences." Easy, but not cheap or painless. When two become one flesh, it is always painful for that flesh to be torn apart. That's what divorce does. It also affects the friends and family of that couple, but most severely, the children from that marriage and for several generations. But, as much as it depends on you, keep peace with your spouse and try to keep the marriage together.

It is the man who is primarily responsible for the marital oneness and the leadership in the family (Eph 5:23). As you began courting your wife, she became the focal point of your life and now she must be the priority above your friends or other family. She has to know beyond any doubt that she comes first with you, that is what makes her feel most "one" with you. But, as previously discussed, that does not mean the man is to lord it over his wife, he is to lead by example and serve his wife as well. He will be held accountable by God.

In his book "His Needs, Her Needs", Willard Harley lists ten most common needs that both men and women have in a marital relationship. Typically, there will be four or five needs that are more important to the man (sexual fulfillment, recreational companionship, an attractive spouse, domestic support, and admiration) and the other four or five are more important to the woman (financial security, affection, conversation, trust and family commitment).[k] Even though all ten are important to both, men and women usually prioritize them differently, and when the husband sees that the most important needs of his wife are met, it is amazing how she will find ways to ensure that his needs are also met, but the husband often has to take the initiative to make it all happen because he is the leader.

Infidelity does not have to be the end of a marriage, though it often is. People commonly mistake infidelity as the problem, when it is usually just a very serious symptom. The problem is someone's need is not being met by their spouse, so it leaves that person vulnerable to extramarital sources for fulfillment, such as internet chat rooms, pornography, an office relationship; some kind of search for another partner. You may be especially vulnerable to temptation whenever you are hurt, angry, lonely or tired (HALT). This does not justify infidelity, but when we feel empty inside, we find it easier to rationalize destructive behavior.

Many couples have survived infidelity, but it is not an easy road. Each person must understand their own vulnerabilities that lead to them seeking fulfillment outside the marriage. Then they can communicate their wants, needs and desires to their spouse and work on ways to get those needs met within the marriage and healing can take place. It has happened repeatedly and marriages have been saved!

So now what? If your marriage is troubled and you are nearing the precipice of separation, there is still some hope for renewal and reconciliation. Get counseling! If your spouse won't attend with you, go by yourself. Whether the marriage survives or fails, you must address those issues that are your fault. Own your mistakes, understand how you could have done things better and grow from the experience. If you don't understand and correct the errors from this relationship, you will likely repeat them in the next one. And the next one. And the next one. This is something you need to do whether you stay married or not, for your own personal growth, and it could be the catalyst that demonstrates your renewed commitment to your spouse and saving the marriage

Offer forgiveness and seek it from your spouse. If the marriage ends in divorce, there must still be grieving and healing that takes place. Any time we experience a loss, it must be grieved and understood. Then forgiveness can take place and provide a path for healing. We must be truly sorry for our part in the failed relationship, taking responsibility for our wrongs and seek forgiveness from the person we have hurt. We must forgive ourselves after properly grieving the loss, then move on with our lives without anger or bitterness, but growing from the experience. When you have recovered, you might be very helpful to others who are struggling with the same thing you have been through, offering hope to them and helping them get through a trial you've experienced.

So, what can be done for someone unable to stop the divorce or who is already divorced? There are so many aspects to deal with; there is the loss of a close friend and companion. You might have feelings of rejection, abandonment, anger, bitterness, betrayal, financial burdens and more.

First, you need to make sure you and the kids are safe. Love endures all things, but it does not enable all evil. If there has been abuse in the relationship, there must be physical separation from the abuser until he or she has demonstrated rehabilitation and the abuse will not recur. You may need legal counsel for restraining orders or for the actual separation and division of assets. You may need competent psychological counsel to regain your mental health and become strong enough to recover. Divorce is extremely stressful, even more so than the death of a spouse or moving, because it often involves both the loss and the uprooting components of these.

Get good counsel, both spiritual and legal. Consider a mediator instead of an attorney, especially if both of you can agree on mediation. It should be cheaper, faster and equitable for both. Mediation is a process of finding solutions and compromising, whereas litigation is more about getting revenge and fighting over assets and access to the children. Your divorce attorney is not your friend. It is often the attorneys who are the biggest winners in a hotly contested separation, the spouses may lose all of their assets, be saddled with large legal bills and the kids are torn between two devastated households. The attorneys make sure they get paid first.

Next, find a divorce support group. Many churches use a video series called DivorceCare and will walk with you through all of the stages of recovery. You can support others going through the same experience and learn to understand how and why this has happened. It provides a path for healing and forgiveness, so you can become healthy again and have a better chance of success if you should decide to pursue marriage again. You might learn to choose a spouse more wisely, or become a better parent to your children. There is so much to gain and no risk of embarrassment or shame. It is comforting and uplifting. Typically, you will explore these twelve steps for overcoming the pain of divorce as suggested by Dick Innes:

"Divorce is one of the most painful experiences any family can experience. It's not only the death of a marriage, but also the death of dreams and hopes, and can be more painful than physical death which at least has a sense of finality to it.

Of one thing we can be sure, however, even though God hates divorce (as well as everything else that is harmful to people), he loves divorced people and families and wants them to be healed and made whole. The healing or recovery process may not be easy but it sure beats staying in the valley of despair. So, if we have experienced the tragedy of divorce, how can we recover, grow through it and allow it to make us much healthier persons?

First, **acknowledge the loss**. After the initial shock it's tempting to go into denial either by refusing to face the reality of what has happened or by burying our feelings of hurt, anger and grief. So the first step in recovery is to face the reality of the situation and be truly honest with how we feel.

Second, **accept the pain as being normal**. Pain is nature's way to tell us something is broken and needs fixing. Whether a broken arm or a broken heart, the pain needs to motivate us to get the help we need to heal and to take proper care of ourselves.

Third, **realize that this, too, will pass**. With divorce it is easy to feel that life is over and that we will never love again. However, if we work through the recovery process, the pain will pass and we can come out much healthier and more mature persons.

Fourth, **don't waste your pain, invest it**. The greatest way we can invest our pain is to use it to motivate us to grow and become better persons, and then support others who are going through divorce and help them to see that they, too, can survive and become happier, healthier persons.

Fifth, **give yourself time to heal**. A broken arm takes six weeks to heal. Broken hearts take much longer – but not forever. As we work through the recovery steps, we will heal. For some it may

57

take up to a year or more. But, if we still haven't resolved our pain after say two years, chances are we haven't faced or dealt with our feelings and that is keeping us stuck. If this is your case, I suggest getting professional counsel to help you work through your loss and the recovery process.

Sixth, **do your grieving now**. With all loss there are many emotions such as hurt, anger, guilt, and deep grief – all of which need to be expressed creatively otherwise they will be acted out destructively. Find a safe person to share them with even if it has to be a professional counselor. If we put walls around our negative feelings we also block out our positive feelings. A vital part of the healing process is to weep and even sob out our grief. As Jesus said, "Blessed are those who mourn, for they will be comforted." (Matthew 5:4 NIV)

Seventh, **forgive to be free**. Failing to forgive keeps us bound to the past but to make genuine forgiveness possible, we need to resolve and get rid of all our negative emotions of hurt, anger and grief. Unless we do this, we will take our negative emotions into all our future close relationships.

Eighth, **let go of the past**. I've worked with people who were divorced as long as twenty years ago and were still hanging onto the fantasy that their ex-spouse would return – even though they had remarried. We need to work through our pain, then let go of it. It helps to hand our failures over to God, ask for his forgiveness for our part in the marriage breakup, receive it by faith and then forgive ourselves. Then leave it with God and get on with life.

Ninth, **guard against a rebound**. Rushing into another romantic relationship too soon can cause us to avoid facing the pain of our marriage breakup and then, if we marry before resolving our past, we are destined to repeat it.

Tenth, **get into a support group**. None of us can make it alone. We weren't meant to. We need to be connected to safe, supportive, accepting and non-judgmental people. We got hurt in hurtful relationships and get healed in wholesome relationships. The Bible says, "God sets the lonely in families." (Psalm 68:6 NIV) He does this through other people and the closest thing we can get to a family is a small support and recovery group.

Eleventh, **realize that failure is never final** and that the only real failure is not to get up one more time than we fall down.

Twelfth, **call on God for help**. Any failure or divorce can be "God's wake up call" to show us that we need to get into recovery and grow. Especially pray that God will show you the truth of what you contributed to your marriage breakup and why you were attracted to the person you married in the first place. The danger is that what we don't resolve we are destined to repeat."[1]

Remember that no matter what you have ever done or failed to do, God loves you and wants to make you whole. As his Word says, "Consider it pure joy, my brothers (and sisters), whenever you face trials of many kinds, because you know that the testing of your faith develops perseverance. Perseverance must finish its work so that you may be mature and complete, not lacking anything." (James 1:2-4 NIV)

With God's help, the support of safe friends and working through the recovery process you will find healing from your hurt and a greater measure of wholeness and spiritual enrichment.

Get counseling for the children too, and keep them informed in a positive manner. They will be concerned about both parents, but mostly they want answers to questions about how this is going to affect them. Where will they live, go to school, see relatives, can they have a puppy now? Always reassure them that they are loved by both parents and that they bear no responsibility for the divorce. Don't battle your spouse for their affection, or bad-mouth their other parent. This will only cause them to come to the defense of the attacked parent, because they love you both. Then they will resent you for the attack, whether founded or not. Children don't need the guilt trip, don't use them as pawns. Philip M. Stahl[m] offers these six steps to positive parenting after divorce from his book "Parenting after Divorce":

"When your marriage ends, you still need to take care of your children. Many parents, however, struggle with their own feelings of anger and sadness, and this makes parenting a difficult task. In trying to make up for the loss of the family unit, you may overindulge your children or try to buy love. Or unknowingly you may become victim to your child's manipulation. Take personal responsibility for your job as a parent, meeting your child's needs in the healthiest possible way:

1. **Don't worry about criticism from the other parent**. Criticism is common where hostility during the divorce increases. If your ex criticizes your parenting techniques, think first about whether there is some validity to the criticism. For example, is the bedtime for your child reasonable, are mealtimes predictable, and is discipline appropriate? Ignore baseless criticism.
2. **Take self-responsibility**. You might have negative thoughts and feelings about your ex, but your primary task is to be the best possible parent you can be during the time your child is with you. Pay attention to your own parenting job and attempt to improve it. This will show your children that you love them and are working to be a parent in the healthiest possible way. Don't focus on blaming the other parent.
3. **Be a parent, not a friend**. It's common for a parent to befriend a child during divorce. This makes it difficult for you to discipline or set rules for your child. Also common is to confide more information about your life than the child can handle – an unnecessary burden for the child. At this point, your child needs a parent as never before. So set rules and enforce them, encourage sharing on the child's part concerning feelings or fears.
4. **Discipline and love your child**. Both the adult and child may come to realize that there are different kinds of love and while the parents have fallen out of love, the parent-child relationship continues. The child may worry that your relationship with him or her may end as well. If discipline is not given in a loving manner, your child may feel insecure about your love. Parents often forget to discipline their child in the emotional turmoil of divorce. Setting up rules for and structure to the child's life are so important at this time. By disciplining your child in a healthy way, you are showing him or her that you love him or her. By showing your child love and positive attention, you reduce the need to punish. (Proverbs 29:17)
5. **Avoid your child's blackmail**. When parents divorce and their children spend time in two different homes, it is easy for them to

pit one parent against the other. Your child might do this – maybe unconsciously – to encourage you and your ex to be in contact with one another in the hope that the two of you might get back together. However, your child also can become mercenary at times, demanding things from each of you. In a divorce situation, parents often are competitive with each other and cave in to the child's demands. It's easy to worry that your child will love the other parent more than you. Remember, your child will come to respect you if you set limits.

6. **Remain flexible**. When dealing with transportation between two households, and the rules in each, it is difficult to have a single set of rules or a sense of direction or wholeness. Your child must adapt and comply with two homes – no easy task. You can help your child by being flexible in your demands from the child – and your ex."

If you have already messed up, when things look hopeless and confusing, do the NEXT RIGHT THING. You can't change the past, but you can resolve to start doing things right from this moment on. Do the next right thing and begin to put the broken pieces of your life back together. When you seek to do what is right in the eyes of God, He will be with you through the restoration and healing process. Find counseling, whether alone or together you will need it; whether the marriage survives or fails, you will need it; and find a recovery and support group if you are divorced.

Resources:

"Choosing Wisely Before You Divorce" DVD series by Family Life Today with Steve Grissom www.fltoday.org

"How We Love – A Revolutionary Approach to Deeper Connections in Marriage" by Milan & Kay Yerkovich © 2006, Waterbrook Press, A division of Random House Inc., 12265 Oracle Blvd., Suite 200, Colorado Springs, CO 80921 (Get the workbook also!)

"Love and Respect – The Love She Most Desires, The Respect He Desperately Needs." by Dr. Emerson Eggerichs © 2004 Integrity Publishers, 5250 Virginia Way, Suite 110, Brentwood, TN 37027

"Boundaries in Marriage - When to say yes, when to say no." by Drs. Henry Cloud and John Townsend © 1999 Zondervan Publishing House, Grand Rapids, MI 49530

"Safe People - How to find relationships that are good for you and avoid those that aren't" by Drs. Henry Cloud and John Townsend © 1995 Zondervan Publishing House, Grand Rapids, MI 49530

"Boundaries Face to Face – How to have that difficult conversation you've been avoiding" by Drs. Henry Cloud and John Townsend © 2003 Zondervan Publishing House, Grand Rapids, MI 49530

"God Will Make A Way – What To Do When You Don't Know What To Do" by Drs. Henry Cloud and John Townsend © 2002 Integrity Publishers, 5250 Virginia Way, Suite 110, Brentwood, TN 37027

"Changes that Heal –How to Understand Your Past to Ensure a Healthier Future" by Dr. Henry Cloud © 1990, 1992 Zondervan Publishing House, Grand Rapids, MI 49530

"How People Grow – What the Bible Reveals about Personal Growth" by Drs. Cloud and Townsend © 2001 Zondervan Publishing House, Grand Rapids, MI 49530

"Hiding from Love: How to change the withdrawal patterns that isolate and imprison you" by Dr. John Townsend © 1991, 1996 Zondervan Publishing House, Grand Rapids, MI 49530

"His Needs, Her Needs – Building An Affair-proof Marriage" by Willard F. Harley, Jr. © 1986, 1994 Fleming H. Revell, a division of Baker Book House Company, P.O. Box 6287, Grand Rapids, MI 49516

"Surviving an Affair" by Drs. Willard F. Harley, Jr. and Jennifer Harley Chalmers © 1998 Baker Publishing Group, P.O. Box 6287, Grand Rapids, MI 49516

"Every Woman's Marriage - Igniting the joy & passion you both desire" by Shannon & Greg Ethridge © 2006 Waterbrook Press, A division of Random House Inc., 12265 Oracle Blvd., Suite 200, Colorado Springs, CO 80921

"Every Man's Marriage – Every Man's Guide to… Winning the Heart of a Woman"* by Steven Arterburn, Fred Stoeker & Mike Yorkey © 2001 Waterbrook Press, A division of Random House Inc., 2375 Telstar Drive, Suite 160, Colorado Springs, CO 80920

*"Every Woman's Desire" has been retitled and released as "Every Man's Marriage"

"The God of Second Chances – Experiencing His Grace for the Rest of Your Life" by Stephen Arterburn © 2002 Thomas Nelson Publishers, Nashville, TN

"New Life after Divorce - The Promise of Hope Beyond Pain" by Bill Butterworth © 2005 Waterbrook Press, 2375 Telstar Drive, Suite 160, Colorado Springs, CO 80920

"The Promise of the Second Wind – It's Never Too Late to Pursue God's Best" by Bill Butterworth & Dean Merrill © 2003 Waterbrook Press, 2375 Telstar Drive, Suite 160, Colorado Springs, CO 80920

"The Worn Out Woman – When Your Life is Full and Your Spirit is Empty" by Dr. Steve Stephens and Alice Gray © 2004 Multnomah Publishers, Inc., P.O. Box 1720, Sisters, OR 97759

"The Walk Out Woman – When Your Heart is Empty and Your Dreams are Lost" by Dr. Steve Stephens and Alice Gray © 2004 Multnomah Publishers, Inc., P.O. Box 1720, Sisters, OR 97759

"Breaking the Cycle of Divorce – How your marriage can succeed even if your parents' didn't" by Dr. John Trent © 2006 Tyndale House Publishers, Carol Stream, IL 60188

"Love Must Be Tough – New Hope for Families in Crisis" by Dr. James Dobson © 1996 Word Publishing, Thomas Nelson Publishers, Nashville, TN

"When Bad Things Happen to Good Marriages How to stay together when life pulls you apart" by Drs. Les and Leslie Parrott © 2001 Zondervan Publishing House, Grand Rapids, MI 49530

"When Your Marriage Dies - Answers to questions about separation and divorce" by Laura Petherbridge © 2005 Cook Communications Ministries, Colorado Springs, CO

Movie "A Vow to Cherish" (© 1999) available on VHS and DVD

Websites:

www.newlife.com — Free tips, helpful books, videos, radio show archives

www.family.org — Free articles, links, resources

www.familylife.com — Family Life Today, Dennis Rainey &

	Bob Lepine
www.fltoday.com	Family Life Today
www.marriagebuilders.com	Marital solutions
www.southeastchristian.org	Church with counseling resources in Louisville, KY
www.troubledwith.com	Focus on the Family helpsite
www.divorcecare.com	Divorce recovery and support for adults and children
www.dc4k.org/about/	DivorceCare for kids
1-800-NEWLIFE	Toll-free helpline and counselors in your area.
1-800-FLTODAY	Family Life Today toll-free helpline
"Weekend to Remember"	conferences - www.familylife.com. conferences/default.asp

Chapter 5 – Addictive Behaviors

It is amazing to me that there are so many things that can be addicting. Recently, I have found myself addicted to Andy Capp's Hot Chili Cheese Steak Fries. Fortunately, that's not a terribly destructive addiction, and I can quit any time I want. Really! But true, out-of-control addictions require a change of lifestyle or an intervention. Some of our more serious and destructive addictions are illegal drugs, prescription drugs, alcohol, tobacco products (nicotine), even food if we are overeating in response to an unfulfilled need in our lives. These are all ingestive addictions, but there are behavioral addictions as well. We can be addicted to love, sex, gambling, shopping, spending, video games and many other behaviors. Yet most of these things are acceptable at times, like taking appropriate drugs when you are sick, drinking alcoholic beverages in moderation, shopping at Home Depot, and we all need to eat! So how do we know if we have crossed the line from normal to addictive behavior? There are some signs we can look for (from New Life tips):

If the behavior becomes obsessive, consuming more of your time at the expense of other activities.
If you feel ashamed or need to hide the behavior from others, especially your spouse.
If you keep a personal stash for "emergency" use.

If your normal performance level is suffering from the behavior.

If the behavior is causing financial difficulties.

If the behavior has you in social isolation.

These are some clues that might indicate we have crossed the line. Certainly, getting the opinion of trusted friends and relatives may confirm a problem, (unless you have cut off all of your past connections to avoid accountability).

Rush Limbaugh has been treated for an addiction to prescription painkillers, but this addiction may have gone on for years had it not been exposed, that is the nature of addiction! It can happen to anyone, but there is tremendous success in treatment today because we understand the nature of addiction and the path to recovery for life!

Gambling Addiction

Here's a quick self-test: 14 Questions Every Gambler Should Ask, from the book "Turning the Tables on Gambling" by Gregory L. Jantz.

Answer these questions honestly and open your heart to God.

1. Consider the things in your life of value to you. They can include family and friends, activities you enjoy or find meaningful. How much time do you devote to each of these valuable things?
2. How much time do you devote to gambling during a week? Contrast that amount of time with the time you put down for the valuable things in your life.
3. Think about how you feel when you gamble. Are those feelings negative or positive? If they are negative, consider why you engage in an activity that promotes negative feelings. If they are positive, how long do those positive feelings last? Do they outlast the gambling activity itself, or do they dissipate as soon as you have stopped gambling?
4. With busy lives, often decisions must be made about how to spend our time. Think back over the past six months. How many times has a decision about whether to gamble come up against

a need to do another activity? This could be time spent with family or friends, time spent working, even time spent relaxing or sleeping. How often has gambling won out over these other things and at what cost?

5. When you think back over your gambling, does it seem like you enjoyed it more at the beginning or now? If it has changed over time, can you remember when the transition occurred?

6. Do you feel isolated from your family or friends when you gamble? Do you feel as if they are unable to understand the way you feel about it? If they are out of touch with gambling, do you feel they are out of touch with you?

7. When other people have questioned you about your gambling, how have you felt? Do you feel they are invading your privacy by questioning you? Do you feel defensive about your gambling?

8. How honest have you been with others about how much time you spend gambling and/or how much money you spend gambling? Do you find yourself trying to hide or cover up the truth about your gambling?

9. When you are in the midst of gambling, do you ever feel like you are getting away with something? How does that make you feel? Bad? Excited?

10. Consider your gambling over the past six months. Now consider your spirituality over the past six months. Has your gambling increased and your spirituality decreased? Have you missed your connection with God? Would you be willing to alter your gambling behavior if it meant being closer to God?

11. Think about all of the things gambling promises. Honestly evaluate how much of a motivation those things are in your life. Do you desire them too much? Is gambling really the way to achieve them?

12. When you are gambling, do you engage in activities you feel guilty about? Do you drink or smoke excessively while gambling? Do you flirt or engage in sexual conversations with other gamblers? Does gambling strengthen your resolve to live a godly life or does it weaken you?

13. If you had to give up gambling or your loved ones tomorrow, which would you choose? Having chosen to give up the first

thing - gambling - did you still wish you could somehow continue to have both? Were you relieved it was only a question and not a reality?

14. If you had to give up gambling or God tomorrow, which one would you choose? Have you made this choice already?[n]

Food Addictions

One of the side effects of living in a prosperous nation like ours is a tendency toward obesity. I have seen, just in my lifetime, that we are becoming an overweight people in alarming numbers. The average passenger weight used to calculate the weight of a commercial jet for takeoff has been increased by the FAA. Stadium seats have been made wider to accommodate our increasing width. Access to plentiful food and making a living without manual labor has a tendency to increase the average weight of the citizens. Failing to restrain our appetites for high fat, sugar and carbohydrate foods, coupled with a population exercising less, will always lead to expanding our waistlines.

We spend billions of dollars on hamburgers, fries, soft drinks and diet books. Yet the solution is not so much what we are eating, it is how much we are eating, and WHY we are eating. Most of us are NOT eating because we are hungry, and we are not stopping when our hunger should be satisfied. We are not eating out of physical need; we are overeating to feed our emotional and spiritual hunger. If you truly want to lose weight and keep it off for life; if you want to be a happier, healthier person, you need to read "Lose It for Life" by Steve Arterburn and Dr. Linda Mintle. They have helped hundreds with their total solution – spiritual, emotional and physical – for permanent weight loss. They also conduct the Lose It for Life Workshops. Find out more at www.loseitforlife.com. Dr. Mintle has also written a book aimed at healthier eating and lifestyle for our kids titled "Overweight Kids"

Here is a brief test for other eating disorders:

1. Do you make yourself sick because you feel uncomfortably full?

2. Do you worry you have lost control over how much you eat?
3. Have you recently lost more than 15 pounds in a three-month period?
4. Do you believe yourself to be fat when others say you are too thin?
5. Would you say that food dominates your life?

If you answered "yes" to two or more of these questions, you may be suffering from anorexia, bulimia or bingeing. These are some of the issues that are treated at Remuda Ranch, www.remuda-ranch.com

Sexual Addictions - These will be dealt with in depth in Chapter Six on Sexual Integrity.

Shopping – We will deal with that in Chapter Ten on Finances.

Drs. Henry Cloud and John Townsend offer these 20 Steps to Defeating Addictions from their book "God Will Make a Way":

"It does not matter what you are addicted to.
It does not matter how long you have been addicted.
It does not matter how severe the consequences.

If you are willing to allow God to make a way, He will. All you have to do is to stop trying to tell yourself to be strong, admit that you are weak, and get into His system of recovery. You will notice that many of them are the same as the twelve steps of Alcoholics Anonymous. The plan works if you work the plan. The strength will not come from you but from God. Yet you have to go to Him with your weakness and join His program in order to receive His strength. We encourage you to do that and to discover, like millions before you, that no matter what you have lost, God can make a way.

1. Admit to yourself, to God, and to another person that you are out of control and this addiction has gotten the best of you. Admit that you are powerless on your own to fix it.
2. Ask God for forgiveness for whatever you have done, and claim it. Receive it, and get rid of all condemnation.

3. Believe that God can help you, reach out to Him, and totally submit yourself to His care, guidance, direction, and strength. Submit to total obedience to whatever He shows you to do.

4. Take an ongoing inventory of all that is wrong inside and between you and others, and all that you have done wrong. Confess it to God and to someone you can trust and be vulnerable with.

5. Continually ask God to show you anything that you need to work on, and when He tells you, follow through.

6. Go and ask for forgiveness and make amends to all whom you have hurt, except where that might harm the person.

7. Seek God deeply, ask Him what He wants you to do, ask Him for the power to do it, and then follow through in obedience.

8. Reach out to others.

9. Find out the triggers that get your addictive behavior started, and then when they occur, reach out. Do not ever underestimate the need to reach out. That is why some addicts especially in the beginning, go to multiple meetings every day and have a sponsor whom they can call.

10. Discover the hurts and pains that you are trying to medicate and seek to have them healed. Find out what you are lacking inside and begin to reach out and receive the love and strengthening that you need.

11. Do not try to do all of this alone. Join a support system, maybe attending every day for a few months, and get a few buddies to call on every day.

12. Find out what relational skills you need to develop in order to make your relationships work. Work on these skills and take risks in order to relate to people better.

13. Forgive everyone who has ever hurt you.

14. Find your talents and develop them. Pursue your dreams and goals.

15. Simplify your life so that it has less stress, and make sure that you are recreating and taking care of yourself.

16. Join a structured group that is going to provide the discipline to do all of this.

17. Study God's Word and other spiritual writings that will teach you how to apply it.

18. Stay humble, be honest, and remember that spiritual growth and recovery are for a lifetime, not just for a season.
19. If you are addicted to a substance, seek medical help as well. In the beginning it is possible that you will go through withdrawal or other serious medical conditions. Make sure that you are safe.
20. See your addiction not as the problem but as a symptom of a life that is not planted and growing in God. Get into recovery as a life overhaul, not just to fix a symptom."°

Drug and Alcohol Addictions

Part of the problem with these addictions is the secrecy and denial that accompanies them, that is one of the symptoms. These addictions must be dealt with professionally and in community with others in recovery. Calvary Center has an experienced staff and excellent track record for successfully beating these addictions. Alanon, Alateen and Alcoholics Anonymous meetings are widely available and Celebrate Recovery can be found in about three thousand churches across the United States. For our pilot group, every airline has a drug and alcohol awareness program, and pilots who self-disclose and complete treatment are protected from job loss, but you must come forward *voluntarily!* If you are discovered by random testing or get a DUI on the road, you are not protected and are risking your career. It isn't worth it! Spouses: If you KNOW your pilot spouse has a drug or alcohol problem, protect yourself and them by urging them to seek treatment and recovery! It's even covered by insurance at most airlines. If your spouse gets caught, it's GAME OVER! Just ask the former America West pilots who were convicted recently. Fortunately, this is not a massive problem in our pilot population, but public safety demands "no tolerance" when help is so widely available. Most pilots know better than to get involved in illegal drugs and marijuana, but we also need to be vigilant for prescription drug abuse from painkillers to sleeping pills. Even over-the-counter medications can cause problems.

Finding a good counselor:

Counselors can not provide quick fixes, but that is what everyone wants. Most people have spent years packing their baggage or hiding their addictions. A good counselor must patiently assess the situation and the client usually needs time and experience with the counselor to feel trusting and willing to work through the recovery process, which may be a matter of months or years depending on the severity of the problem, the social environment and the desire of the person to succeed in recovery. It is an experience that the client must internalize to make it a lifelong change of behavior. The experienced counselor will always be looking for something else that may be contributing to the problem as well. There are usually multiple links in the chain of addiction.

Some common mistakes counselors might make are premature problem solving, interrogating, passing moral judgment, impatience, setting personal limits and being disorganized. If you run into these practices early on or frequently, I would look for a new counselor.

An effective counselor MUST have warmth, genuineness and empathy. While these are necessary, they are not sufficient. An effective counselor must also be an active listener and have a working knowledge of when and how to use practical techniques which are proven helpful in alleviating specific struggles. This comes mostly from years of experience and continuing education.

Interventions

Sometimes an addict will not admit the problem until he hits rock bottom or is confronted by those who love him in a way that removes his ability to live in denial. This is an intervention. With the help of the good counselor you found above, s/he will arrange the time and place for the intervention. The addict will be faced with the people closest to him and confronted with his behavior. He will be made to listen to all of these witnesses present at the same time, how he has hurt them and disappointed them repeatedly. These can be his children if they are emotionally mature enough to participate, but will usually be limited to the spouse, parents, siblings, the counselor, the addicts' pastor if there is one, perhaps a current or former boss (if it will not further jeopardize his career), and close friends who will love him and support him in recovery, but are drawing the line on their relationship until he gets help. Everyone will emphasize that they are FOR the person and against the addiction.

Usually, the reaction is anger, frustration and running away. The more people present, the less likely it will be a violent reaction and there will be no hiding from the evidence and testimony of all of these people who have his best interest in mind. Sometimes, the reaction is deep pain, sorrow and repentance. That is the goal. That is the first step to seeking rescue from the addiction that is beyond his ability to control. That is a positive step toward healing, forgiveness and growth. He will need all of you to love him through the recovery process. He will have to work hard and be patient as he tries to rebuild trust in the damaged relationships, but you can support him as you hold him accountable and see how God can restore everything that was lost. Help him to do the next right thing.

Resources:

"Helping the Struggling Adolescent - A Guide to Thirty-Six Common Problems for Counselors, Pastors, and Youth Workers" by Dr. Les Parrott III © 1993, 2000 Zondervan, Grand Rapids, MI 49530 (With 43 Rapid Assessment Tests)

"How People Grow" What the Bible Reveals about Personal Growth" by Drs. Cloud and Townsend © 2001 Zondervan Publishing House, Grand Rapids, MI 49530

"The Life Recovery Bible"- NLT 12-step recovery program, topical index and devotionals for anyone in recovery by Stephen Arterburn and David Stoop © 2006 Tyndale House Publishers, Carol Stream, IL 60188

"Transformation – Turn Your Life Around Starting Today" by Stephen Arterburn and David Stoop © 1998, 2006 Tyndale House Publishers, Carol Stream, IL 60188

"Lose It for Life – The Total Solution – Spiritual, Emotional, Physical - for Permanent Weight Loss" by Stephen Arterburn and Dr. Linda Mintle © 2004 Integrity Publishers, 5250 Virginia Way, Suite 110, Brentwood, TN 37027

"Lose It for Life for Teens – Find and Maintain Your Right Weight for Life" by Stephen Arterburn & Ginger Garrett, The Spiritual,

Emotional, & Physical Solution © 2004 Integrity Publishers, 5250 Virginia Way, Suite 110, Brentwood, TN 37027

"Overweight Kids" by Dr. Linda Mintle This positive, practical and inspirational guide will help parents find spiritual and behavioral solutions to help their overweight child. © 2005 Thomas Nelson Publishers, Nashville, TN

"Making Peace with Your Thighs - Get Off the Scales and Get On with Your Life"** by Dr. Linda Mintle © 2006 Thomas Nelson Publishers, Nashville, TN

"Feeding your Appetites - Take Control of What's Controlling You" by Stephen Arterburn and Debra Cherry. Money, Food, Sex, Work, Ego…What God Intends for Good Can Be the Greatest Enemy of a Healthy, Joyful Life. Satisfy your wants, needs and desires without compromising yourself © 2004 Integrity Publishers, 5250 Virginia Way, Suite 110, Brentwood, TN 37027

"Healing is a Choice – Ten Decisions That Will Transform Your Life & Ten Lies That Can Prevent You From Making Them" by Stephen Arterburn © 2005 Thomas Nelson Publishers, Nashville, TN

Soul Care Ministry - Southeast Christian Church in Louisville, KY http://soulcare.southeastchristian.org

New Life Clinics – counseling	www.newlife.com
Lose It for Life – workshops and support	www.loseitforlife.com
Calvary Center – drug & alcohol addictions www.newlife.com
Exodus (drug) Recovery Young men 13-17	www.exodusrecovery.org
Remuda Ranch – Anorexia, Bulimia and eating disorders	www.remudaranch.com
Gambling	www.gamblingexposed.org
Gam-Anon	www.gam-anon.org
Gamblers Anonymous	www.gamblersanonymous.org
Aviation Medicine	www.aviationmedicine.com
Alcoholics Anonymous	www.aa.org
Alanon/Alateen	www.al-anon.org Adult and teenage alcohol recovery

74

Celebrate Recovery   www.celebraterecovery.com Support
                            groups in your area

1-800-gambler
1-800-NewLife

Chapter 6 – Sexual integrity

"THE TROUBLED NORTH AFRICAN man entered the family garden. Despite his mother's ceaseless prayers, he was caught up in a lusty lifestyle, and he couldn't seem to break the cycle. Although he longed for a relationship with God, he was unable to stop his self-destructive behavior.

He heard the sound of children's voices chanting, "Pick it up, read it; pick it up, read it." Briefly distracted from his misery, the young man wondered what kind of game would cause the children to sing such an odd verse. All at once it occurred to him that perhaps God was sending him a message through their playful words.

He eagerly opened the Bible and began to read: *"Not in rioting and drunkenness, not in chambering and wantonness, not in strife and envying. But put ye on the Lord Jesus Christ, and make no provision for the flesh, to fulfill the lusts thereof. Him that is weak in the faith receive"* (Rom. 13:13—14:1 KJV).

The young man was filled with hope and yearning. He believed that God had given him a passage to assure him that divine power could and would overcome his human weakness.

He rushed into the house and told his mother, Monica—she was filled with incredible joy and wonder. Her prayers had been answered. The young man's life was transformed. Today, he is remembered as St. Augustine.

When young Augustine walked through the garden, he was in prayer. And his mother, Monica, was praying too. Both were expecting answers; both were listening for direction. When the children's words led Augustine to the Scriptures, he found what he was looking for. God met him in his need; He met Monica in her concern. And He transformed a lustful young man into one of the great fathers of the early church—all in response to prayer." - Excerpted from "The Power Book" by Stephen Arterburn

"Giving away virginity is like Esau giving up his birthright to Jacob (Israel). Now Israel is a nation and Esau a footnote. He gave up something so valuable for something so temporary as a bowl of stew and some bread." - Dave Stone, Preaching Minister, Southeast Christian Church

Why is Viagra one of the best selling drugs in the world? And now there is Cialis and Levitra because other drug companies want the billions in profits from these sexual goldmines. Are these phenomenal sales legitimate? Are there really that many men suffering from erectile dysfunction? I don't think so; I think the majority of sales are for "recreational" use to promote increased sexual ability without restraint. This leads to more aggressive behavior, the spread of STD's and a general decline in our society's moral values. Scott Peterson had Viagra in his possession when he was arrested for murdering his wife Laci and son Connor. It was also reported that he ordered pornographic channels in the days right after her disappearance, and we later found out about his adultery. Clearly, this was a man unable or unwilling to control his lust. It has already cost him his freedom and it may cost him his life. We also have reports of convicted sex offenders obtaining paid prescriptions of Viagra at taxpayer expense through Medicaid. I think there is more "recreational" use than true E. D. diagnoses. Rush Limbaugh calls it defining deviancy down, where more and more abhorrent and deviant behavior becomes the new lowered standard for society. We are rapidly cycloning down the moral abyss. Virginity is rarely given value among teenagers today.

God set the standard for all of us: not a hint of immorality. Do not covet your neighbor's wife. Do not commit adultery. Isn't having lust in your heart the definition of coveting? Jesus simply clarified the Torah definition, He did not change it, the Pharisees tried to do that. Jesus said: *"But I tell you that anyone who looks at a woman* *lustfully has **already committed adultery** with her in his heart."* NIV Matthew 5:28 So how far is our society from God's standard? Most of our society isn't even aware there IS a standard.

Here are "10 Red Flags That You May be Struggling with Impurity" (for men) from "Every Man's Battle" by Stephen Arterburn and Fred Stoeker:

"Do you still have a hint of impurity in your life? Some of these red flags could be flapping around the backyard of your life.
1. Do you tell off-color jokes or like coming up with double entendres?
2. Do you channel-surf hoping to glimpse something racy on television?
3. If a certain person at your work calls in sick, do you feel a little down in the dumps?
4. Do you linger over lingerie ads in the paper?
5. Do you watch women's figure skating or women's beach volleyball although you have little interest in the sports?
6. Do you flirt—and know you're doing it?
7. Do you lock on when you see an attractive person?
8. Do you look forward to going on a business trip?
9. Do you have secrets that you can't share with your spouse?
10. Do you think about old flames when things aren't going well at home?"

Here's another test you can take. You don't need a pencil; you just need to be honest with yourself. Answer "yes" or "no" to the following questions:

New Life Ministries Sex Addict Test by Stephen Arterburn (for men and women)
1. Do you lock on when an attractive woman or man comes near you?
2. Do you masturbate to images of other women or men?
3. Have you found your spouse to be less sexually satisfying?
4. Are you holding a grudge against your spouse - a grudge that gives you a sense of entitlement?

5. Do you seek out sexually arousing articles or photo spreads in newspapers or magazines?
6. Do you have a private place or secret compartment that you keep hidden from your spouse?
7. Do you look forward to going away on a business trip?
8. Do you have behaviors that you can't share with your spouse?
9. Do you frequent porn-related sites on the Internet?
10. Do you watch R-rated movies, sexy videos, or steamy cable channels for gratification?

If you've answered "yes" to any of these questions, you're lurking at the door of sexual addiction. You're inside that door if you can answer "yes" to the following questions:

1. Do you watch pay-per-view sexually explicit TV channels at home or on the road?
2. Do you purchase pornography on the Internet?
3. Do you rent adult movies?
4. Do you watch nude dancing?
5. Do you call 900-numbers to have phone sex?
6. Do you practice voyeurism?

If you said "yes" to the last six questions, you very well could be sexually addicted. When Titus 2:3 admonishes against being "addicted to much wine," the Greek word used for "addicted" means to be brought into bondage, much like a slave.

Today we are bombarded with sexual imagery and innuendo from every form of media devised by man. Books, magazines, billboards, TV shows, commercials, movies, advertising, and the Internet. It is the next step for the iPod. We have been so numbed by exposure to racy ads and foul language that most people don't even recognize immoral sexual content unless it is so blatant and in-your-face you CAN'T miss it! Because sex sells.

Hey, it's not hurting anyone, what's the big deal? Does God see sexual sin any differently than other types of sin? Actually, He does. Here's why, 1Cor 6:18-20 (NIV) says: Flee from sexual immorality.

All other sins a man commits are outside his body, but he who sins sexually, sins against his own body. Do you not know that your body is a temple of the Holy Spirit, who is in you, whom you have received from God? You are not your own; you were bought at a price. Therefore honor God with your body.

Temptations from pornography or internet chat rooms chip away at marriage and create unreal expectations and fantasies. Pornography is wrong. It stimulates lust, it pollutes the mind, it funds sinful behavior, it alienates couples with secrecy or disappointment, it is addictive, it numbs the senses and it violates the covenant of forsaking all others. It leaves you with an image of "perfect" no real person can compare to and sets you up for disappointment in any real relationship. It destroys marriages and families.

From "Helping the Struggling Adolescent" by Dr. Les Parrott III, "Violent pornography champions the notion that sexual violence, usually directed against women, is normal. Degrading pornography debases and dehumanizes women even if the material does not depict explicit violent behavior. The general definition of Langly Longford is: Pornography is that which exploits and dehumanizes sex, so that human beings are treated as things, and women in particular as sex objects."

He goes on to report: "Several lines of evidence show that in many sex crimes, pornography has been among the triggering influences – especially in cases of rape. Pornography promotes the myth that women want to be raped. As one researcher put it, "Pornography promotes a climate in which acts of sexual hostility directed against women are not only tolerated ideologically, but encouraged."

Pornography contributes to unrealistic expectations about sexuality, and its addictiveness destroys real life relationships, often consuming hours at a time, wasting productivity or more wholesome family activity. I think the proliferation of pornography has lead to the increase we have seen in child kidnappings, rapes and murders, along with a general devaluation of human life in this country.

How big is the problem? The pornography industry in the U. S. is bigger than the revenue taken in by the NFL, NHL, NBA and MLB *combined!* It is also the driving force behind lewd and violent music videos. Free radio stations inundate our kids (and some parents!) with vulgar, sexual, crude and violent lyrics and shock jocks. Placing parental warnings on packaging hasn't reduced demand, many people today download music; there is no packaging. The video game industry targets teens and twenties with sexually explicit and violent games that waste our time and our minds. So what can we do about it? Don't buy it! Get involved in setting community standards in your city, with local churches. Cincinnati has been successful in eradicating commercial pornography from within its limits by shutting down nude bars, and ending the sales of explicit sexual materials. Louisville is beginning a similar campaign through churches, the mayors and city councils, and holding our elected officials accountable for the businesses they allow to operate within their districts. (Louisville actually has several smaller cities within its recently merged city and county governments.)

Watch what your kids are exposed to in all facets of the media and make sure they are monitored when using the internet. Use tamperproof filtering software that records and emails to you all sites visited and prevents inappropriate viewing. Use "V" chip technology on your cable or satellite receiver to block entire channels or shows with inappropriate content. Listen to the songs your kids like, look for the lyrics on the internet. Hold yourself to the same standards and don't allow that stuff into your home and mind. If you struggle with this addiction, get counseling and get healthy. You can save your marriage, your dignity, your children and the consequences of pornography as soon as you admit there is a problem. Help is available.

10 Steps to Overcoming Pornography Addiction from Steve Arterburn

"1. First, you must acknowledge the addiction exists. Many who are caught in the trap of addiction will adamantly deny the problem. *He who conceals his transgressions will not prosper, but he who confesses and forsakes them will find compassion.* - Proverbs 28:13

2. You must recognize that what you are doing is wrong. Addicts find a way to justify their problem in their mind. *For all that*

is in the world, the lust of the flesh and the lust of the eyes and the boastful pride of life, is not from the Father, but is from the world. - I John 2:16

3. You must not blame others - "If my wife/husband were just more affectionate." ... "If women/men were not so seductive." Adam blamed Eve and she blamed the serpent. Instead, you must begin to take responsibility for your actions.

4. Make yourself accountable to a spiritual authority, perhaps a pastor or mature believer. Everybody needs a "safe" person to share their struggles with. *Therefore, confess your sins to one another and pray for one another, so that you may be healed. The effective prayer of a righteous man can accomplish much.* - James 5:16

5. You must recognize that "will power" is not the answer. At a weak moment, your "will" may fail you. By admitting that you are in need of God's help, you open access to His supernatural intervention in your life. You must yield your will to God's will. That's when He can begin a new work in your life.

6. Study the Word of God concerning sexual purity. *Therefore putting aside all filthiness and all that remains of wickedness, in humility receive the Word implanted, which is able to save your souls.* - James 1:21

7. You must destroy any pornography in your possession. You can't wean yourself off pornography. Think of the hidden pornography in your home as a ticking time bomb that will ultimately destroy your family.

8. You must learn to flee temptation. Self-deception may enter when you think you can play with fire without getting burned. *Do not enter the path of the wicked, and do not proceed in the way of evil men. Avoid it, do not pass by it. Turn away from it and pass on.* - Proverbs 4:14,15

9. Give yourself time to work through the process of recovery. More often than not, God chooses to take us through a learning and growing process, that can be very painful. Victory over addiction should be viewed as a marathon, not a sprint.

10. It's cliché, but you must approach your addiction one day at a time. Look for little victories and rejoice in the progress you're

making. Recovery is a cinch by the inch, but a trial by the mile.

When you develop a private world centered on your addiction, it's the privacy that's keeping it intact. Disrupt the privacy of your world, then, and you weaken both it and the addiction it protects. You'll be less inclined to repeat the behavior you've given up if you know someone else is involved in your struggle with you.

A trained Christian professional with experience treating addictions will be valuable to you. As always, you should get a referral from your pastor or a trusted friend if possible. But do find qualified help. With it, you can understand the roots of your addiction and build up the defenses against destructive actions that have been torn down over the years.

You also should get into a support group—a Christ-centered one—that's geared toward this problem. This provides you with a legitimate emotional outlet for the conflicting feelings you'll experience while you withdraw from your addiction. And finally, get some accountability. To be accountable to someone means to let him in on your struggle and to keep him up on your progress. It's a giving over of your right to privacy to at least one person who has your permission to question you about your day-to-day activities and encourage you when you struggle.

You may balk at this – I certainly did when I was first told that I'd never maintain my integrity unless I got some accountability. But don't kid yourself—your own history by now has taught you that you can't deal with sexually compulsive behavior by yourself."[P]

Do the next right thing. Resolve to do what is right in God's eyes from this day forward. If you stumble, don't give up, just start doing the next right thing and get your life back on track.

To help stem the epidemic, we must educate our children about these dangers. We must teach our boys and girls the value of virginity. They should understand how the best, most special gift you can give your future husband or wife is your virginity, and that is something so intimate it is never shared with anyone else. It is the thing that makes even a new marriage very special and unique, and it improves with time and experience *together!* You might ask your older teenage son or daughter how many sex partners they want their future spouse to have before marrying them? Hopefully, the answer is none, and you can then explore why they feel that way, and how that future spouse is expecting the same thing from your kids. You can only give away your virginity once; make sure it is on your wedding day with a person you trust for the rest of your life! Your spouse will appreciate that gift more than any other wedding present you can give them! Lastly, pray for them and their future spouses, there is nothing more powerful!

Resources:

For Men:
"Every Man's Battle – Every Man's Guide to... Winning the War on Sexual Temptation One Victory at a Time" by Stephen Arterburn, Fred Stoeker, Mike Yorkey © 2000 Waterbrook Press, A division of Random House Inc., 2375 Telstar Drive, Suite 160, Colorado Springs, CO 80920

"Every Young Man's Battle – Strategies for Victory in the Real World of Sexual Temptation" by Stephen Arterburn, Fred Stoeker, Mike Yorkey © 2002 Waterbrook Press, A division of Random House Inc., 2375 Telstar Drive, Suite 160, Colorado Springs, CO 80920

"Preparing Your Son for Every Man's Battle – Honest Conversations About Sexual Integrity" by Stephen Arterburn, Fred Stoeker, Mike Yorkey © 2003 Waterbrook Press, A division of Random House Inc., 2375 Telstar Drive, Suite 160, Colorado Springs, CO 80920

"Every Man's Marriage – Every Man's Guide to... Winning the Heart of a Woman"* by Steven Arterburn, Fred Stoeker & Mike Yorkey © 2001 Waterbrook Press, A division of Random House Inc., 2375 Telstar Drive, Suite 160, Colorado Springs, CO 80920

*"Every Woman's Desire" has been retitled and released as "Every Man's Marriage"

"Every Man's Battle" workshops – weekend seminars for sexual addictions www.everymansbattle.com

For Women:

"Every Woman's Marriage - Igniting the joy & passion you both desire" by Shannon & Greg Ethridge © 2006 Waterbrook Press, A division of Random House Inc., 12265 Oracle Blvd., Suite 200, Colorado Springs, CO 80921

"Every Woman's Battle – Discovering God's Plan for Sexual and Emotional Fulfillment" by Shannon Ethridge © 2003 Waterbrook Press, A division of Random House Inc., 2375 Telstar Drive, Suite 160, Colorado Springs, CO 80920

"Every Young Woman's Battle - Guarding Your Mind, Heart, and Body in a Sex-Saturated World" by Shannon Ethridge & Stephen Arterburn © 2004 Waterbrook Press, A division of Random House Inc., 2375 Telstar Drive, Suite 160, Colorado Springs, CO 80920

"Preparing Your Daughter for Every Woman's Battle – Creative Conversations about Sexual and Emotional Integrity" by Shannon Ethridge © 2005 Waterbrook Press, A division of Random House Inc., 2375 Telstar Drive, Suite 160, Colorado Springs, CO 80920

"Every Heart Restored – A Wife's Guide to Healing in the Wake of a Husband's Sexual Sin" by Steve Arterburn, Fred & Brenda Stoeker, Mike Yorkey © 2004 Waterbrook Press, A division of Random House Inc., 2375 Telstar Drive, Suite 160, Colorado Springs, CO 80920

"Every Heart Restored" workshops – Weekend seminars for partners of those struggling with sexual addictions www.everyheartrestored.com

For Everyone:

"Addicted to "Love" – Understanding Dependencies of the Heart: Romance, Relationships, and Sex" by Stephen Arterburn © 2003 Gospel Light Publications, Ventura, CA

"Feeding your Appetites - Take Control of What's Controlling You" by Stephen Arterburn and Debra Cherry. Money, Food, Sex, Work, Ego...What God Intends for Good Can Be the Greatest Enemy of a Healthy, Joyful Life. Satisfy your wants, needs and desires without compromising yourself © 2004 Integrity Publishers, 5250 Virginia Way, Suite 110, Brentwood, TN 37027

"The Secrets Men Keep – How Men Make Life and Love Tougher Than It Has to Be" by Stephen Arterburn © 2006 Integrity Publishers, 5250 Virginia Way, Suite 110, Brentwood, TN 37027

"Boundaries in Marriage - When to say yes, when to say no." by Drs. Henry Cloud and John Townsend © 1999 Zondervan Publishing House, Grand Rapids, MI 49530

"Safe People - How to find relationships that are good for you and avoid those that aren't" by Drs. Henry Cloud and John Townsend © 1995 Zondervan Publishing House, Grand Rapids, MI 49530

"Home Invasion – Protecting Your Family In a Culture That's Gone Stark Raving Mad" by Rebecca Hagelin © 2005 Nelson Current, Thomas Nelson Publishers, Nashville, TN

Websites:

www.cloudtownsend.com	Drs. Cloud and Townsend resources
www.newlife.com	New Life Ministries resources
www.everymansbattle.com	Every Man's Battle resources from New Life Ministries
www.everywomansbattle.com	Shannon Ethridge's Every Woman's Battle resources
www.family.org	Focus on the Family resources
www.troubledwith.com	Focus on the Family resources
http://pureintimacy.org	Focus on the Family resources

Chapter 7 – Dating

Being single. We all start out that way, and unless our parents arranged a marriage, staying single is our choice. The Apostle Paul had this to say about singleness: NIV 1 Corinthians 7:1-9 It is good for a man not to marry. But since there is so much immorality, each man should have his own wife, and each woman her own husband. The husband should fulfill his marital duty to his wife, and likewise the wife to her husband. The wife's body does not belong to her alone but also to her husband. In the same way, the husband's body does not belong to him alone but also to his wife. Do not deprive each other except by mutual consent and for a time, so that you may devote yourselves to prayer. Then come together again so that Satan will not tempt you because of your lack of self-control. I say this as a concession, not as a command. I wish that all men were (single) as I am. But each man has his own gift from God; one has this gift, another has that. Now to the unmarried and the widows I say: It is good for them to stay unmarried, as I am. But if they cannot control themselves, they should marry, for it is better to marry than to burn with passion.

In his letter to the church at Corinth, Paul is saying it is better to be single than to be married for the purposes of serving God more fully, without distraction or obligation to a family. However, God also commanded us through Adam and Eve to be fruitful and multiply. With over six billion people on the planet now, I think we have fulfilled that command, and Paul is saying that there are some people who are called to singleness to serve God better, and some who are called to be married and raise a family, and each will have different challenges in their roles in the Church.

So there is nothing negative about being single, for some people it is a gift from God. However, if your desire is to be married, that's where dating comes in.

Why should we date? Is dating solely for the purpose of finding a mate? NO! Dating is not about marriage! Dr. Henry Cloud says, "Dating is as much about learning what you need and want, and how you need to grow and change, as it is about finding the "right" person. Dating is not only a wonderful time of life, but also a context for enormous spiritual and personal growth. You learn so much about yourself, others, God, love, spirituality, and life through dating. Done well, it can be fulfilling in and of itself. Done well, it can be one of the most fun and rewarding aspects of your life. Done well, it can lead to a good marriage."[q]

What's the first step? You must be available and healthy to be involved in dating. Forgive me for stating the obvious, but it must be said: If you are currently married, you are not available. If you are married, but separated, you are not available. If your divorce is not final yet, you are not available. If you are living with someone in an intimate relationship, you are not available. If you are too hurt right now to risk dating, you should get healing first. If you are recently divorced or had a long-term relationship end, you need to be in a divorce recovery program to find healing and identify your areas of needed growth, first. If you are at risk for serious depression or other clinical issues, you should see a good professional and work on those first. If you are an alcoholic, you should not go to a bar. If you are a sex addict, or impulsive, and are in danger of high-risk behavior in this realm, you should not be dating. You should be in recovery and get well first.

Once you are available and healthy, you are ready to start exploring the world of dating. Let's start with our attitude toward dating. You are probably not ready to date if you have always demanded that dating was for serious relationships only. These are the starting points from "How to Get a Date Worth Keeping" by Dr. Henry Cloud:

1. See dating as a wonderful time to find out about other people and what they are like.
2. See dating as a wonderful time to find out about yourself and how you need to change.
3. See dating as an end in and of itself.
4. See dating in a way that takes the pressure off.
5. See dating as an opportunity to love and serve others.
6. See dating as an opportunity to grow in skills
7. Promise yourself that you will make no serious commitment for a certain length of time.

13 Steps to Successful Dating from "God Will Make a Way: Personal Discovery Guide" by Drs. Henry Cloud and John Townsend

1. Begin with pursuing God (Matthew 6:25-34) and become the healthiest person you can become.
2. Get your relationship needs met outside the dating context.
3. Learn your patterns (old relationship patterns from your original family, seeking completion for something you lack in yourself, idealistic wishes for yourself, inability to set boundaries, fear of closeness or intimacy) and work on them so you do not repeat them.
4. Date according to a few non-negotiable values (faith, honesty, sexual purity, etc.). Avoid vileness, faithlessness, perversity, slander, evil, pride, deceit, and lying.
5. Expand your tastes. Be open to going out with people who you would normally not have on your list.
6. Be yourself from the beginning. Don't adapt to what you think the other person will like. Be who you are and give the other person the freedom to do the same.
7. Don't put up with bad behavior, and set good boundaries.
8. Take your time. You would not allow a stranger into your house without proper identification, but many people allow virtual strangers into their hearts, minds, souls, and bodies.

9. Stay connected in other relationships. Members of your support system are the ones who are most objective about the people you are dating.
10. Get active. Network with friends and family; pursue the things you enjoy, join others who have the same need, use your gift of hospitality, and do something structured.
11. Look in the mirror. Is something about your personality, behavior, or the way you come across to others getting in the way of meeting people?
12. Keep yourself sexually pure. Honor sex as something holy and keep it confined to the marriage relationship.
13. Abide in God – and have fun! God is the one who will make a way, so walk with him daily. Pray about your dating life and ask him what he wants you to do.

Some specific tips for women:

If you are using sensuality to attract a man, you will get a man who is attracted to sensuality, not someone who sees how wonderful *you* are. He will be attracted to sensuality wherever he sees it, so don't be surprised when he leaves you for something or someone *more* sensual than you have to offer.

Good men look for the natural beauty of the real woman shining through, the sex appeal that comes from the radiance of a woman's personality, strength, humor, playfulness, virtue, and other things of good character. Healthy men look for a spark and an openness that says "I like you and I am not mad at you for being a man." These things don't diminish with age and can't be altered with surgery. Men want the attractiveness of a woman's real personhood, but for her real personhood to be revealed, it can't be hiding under a lot of health or personal problems.

Many women give themselves to a guy sexually as a way to have the guy like them. They feel that if they sleep with him, he will fall in love with them, and they will finally get the love they need. Nothing is farther from the truth! If a guy loves you, he will wait for you. He will commit to you in marriage. In fact, you may not know whether he truly loves you if he doesn't have to wait for you.

Sex may be the only reason he is around. And most times, they lose respect for you in the process and want to marry someone who is not so "easy." This also demonstrates his lack of self-control.

Some specific tips for men:

Women want a man who is an active initiator, not a passive hoper. They want men to initiate romance both before and after marriage. Nothing is more like a cold shower to a woman, than a man they have to lead around or push into decisions or activity, even when they act as if they would like to control him. Women want a man who is strong and assertive, but who uses that assertiveness in service of the relationship. He doesn't dominate her for selfish reasons. Premarital sex confuses the issues of love and compatibility, because it keeps you from looking at who the woman is you are dating. The sex can be so gratifying that you fail to pay attention to the quality of the relationship apart from sex. It sets you up to be blinded by sex and to make bad choices in women. If there is no sex, you are forced to look at the quality of a woman's character and the kind of relationship you have and to see if she is really someone you want to be attached to. For life.

There are some misconceptions about dating and marriage. These are some things to consider (from "How to Get a Date Worth Keeping")

Are you content with your life? If not, it is not time for marriage.

Are you seeking a relationship to end loneliness? If you are, it won't. Cure your loneliness first.

What are you expecting marriage to provide for you? If you think that it will make you happy when you are not, you are wrong. Unhappy people who get married create unhappy marriages.

Do you see marriage as a romantic fantasy or some other kind of unending bliss? If so, you must get real about marriage. Marriage is a commitment between two imperfect people to love and sacrifice for each other and build something good. So take a hard look at those words – "*commitment, two, imperfect, love, sacrifice,* and *build.*" They all require suffering, effort, delay of gratification, and other painful, character building experiences. The fruit of those experiences can be very, very good. When love is built, it is a very good thing. But it requires work, and it is important that you have a realistic view going into it.

Do you think that marriage is going to make your life significantly better? While marriage can indeed make many things "better," it should not be seen as a way to make your *life* better. If something in your life is not good, fix it. Find a good life as a single. Make it an awesome life. The only kind of person anyone would want to marry anyway is someone with a good life. No one wants to be someone's "solution" for a life that's not working.

Do you want to get married to prove you are okay? Marriage is not going to make you feel okay, nor is it going to make you feel as though you measure up or fit into the rest of society. Marriage does not solve problems that need their own solutions.

The best preparation for marriage is to become a whole, healthy person who does not need to get married. Then you can marry for the right reasons. No one wants to be a rescue mission for someone else; that is not attractive to others.

Listed in the resources at the end of this chapter are "Finding Mr. Right" and "Avoiding Mr. Wrong". Both of these are intended for women looking for the right man, but I highly recommend them for men to read as well, since they can illustrate how we can be Mr. Right or Mr. Wrong.

If you are living with someone you are not married to, stop. Separate until you are married. That's doing the next right thing. Abstain from sex until you are married. If that causes a breakup, you know it was just the sex they were hanging around for. They were just "playing house." Real love is found in real commitment. Living together without the marriage commitment is no commitment at all. Seek to honor God in all of your relationships and you will be blessed.

Choose well during the dating process, and you should never need the chapter on divorce.

Resources:

"How to Get a Date worth Keeping – Be Dating in Six Months or Your Money Back!" by Dr. Henry Cloud *(Money back guarantee!)* © 2005 Zondervan Publishing House, Grand Rapids, MI 49530

"Boundaries in Dating – Making Dating Work" by Drs. Henry Cloud and John Townsend © 2000 Zondervan Publishing House, Grand Rapids, MI 49530

"Safe People - How to find relationships that are good for you and avoid those that aren't" by Drs. Henry Cloud and John Townsend © 1995 Zondervan Publishing House, Grand Rapids, MI 49530

"God Will Make A Way – What To Do When You Don't Know What To Do" by Drs. Henry Cloud and John Townsend © 2002 Integrity Publishers, 5250 Virginia Way, Suite 110, Brentwood, TN 37027

"Finding Mr. Right – (And How To Know When You Have)" by Stephen Arterburn and Dr. Meg J. Rinck © 2001 Thomas Nelson Publishers, Nashville, TN - Plus 10 Ways to Become Mrs. Right

"Avoiding Mr. Wrong – (And What To Do If You Didn't)" by Stephen Arterburn and Dr. Meg J. Rinck © 2000 Thomas Nelson Publishers, Nashville, TN- 10 Men Who Will Ruin Your Life

"The 10 Commandments of Dating – Time-Tested Laws for Building Successful Relationships" by Ben Young and Dr. Samuel Adams © 1999 Thomas Nelson Publishers, Nashville, TN

"Finding the Love of Your Life – Ten Principles for Choosing the Right Marriage Partner" by Dr. Neil Clark Warren © 1992 Pocket Books, A Division of Simon & Schuster Inc., 1230 Avenue of the Americas, New York, NY 10020 Published by arrangement with Focus on the Family Publishing, 8605 Explorer Drive, Colorado Springs, CO 80920

"Falling in Love for all the Right Reasons – How to Find Your Soul Mate" by Dr. Neil Clark Warren © 2005 by eHarmony.com, Time Warner Book Group, 1271 Avenue of the Americas, New York, NY 10020

Websites:

www.cloudtownsend.com   Drs. Cloud and Townsend resources

www.eHarmony.com   Relationship service & resources by

	Dr. Neal Clark Warren
www.newlife.com	New Life Workshop: Singles the Power of One & resources
www.itsjustlunch.com	Dating service for busy professionals
www.troubledwith.com	Focus on the Family general resources
http://pureintimacy.org/	Focus on the Family sexuality resources

Chapter 8 – Disease, Illness and Suffering

If there really is a God, why is there suffering? To help us understand, we need to understand the source of suffering. It is not God. God does allow suffering, and He can use suffering to prepare us for good and noble causes. He can bring us closer to Him and foster maturity through suffering. Growing and teething pains are part of maturing and are good and necessary, even though painful for a child, and those around the suffering child share the emotional struggle.

I recently learned that the Chinese word for crisis is made up of the symbols for danger and opportunity. That is what we see in every crisis, whether a natural disaster like hurricanes, floods and earthquakes, or manmade crises from war and evil governments that refuse to provide food and medicine for citizens, or exterminate groups of people out of hatred like the Holocaust. Each of these has the potential for massive loss of life and suffering, and each have seen the miraculous efforts of people we see as heroes today. Danger and opportunity. Would we ever see the extremes of goodness, mercy and justice, if we never experienced ruthlessness, hardship and injustice? Can we fully appreciate the holiness and love of God if we never experience the unholiness and evil that God allows through Satan?

We see in the Book of Job that God did not cause the suffering Job went through, but allowed Satan to test Job's faith in God through suffering and loss. Job never wavered and passed the test, and God restored all that was lost, even doubling what Job had before he was tested. You see, faith that is not tested is no faith at all. Abraham had his faith tested, so did Jesus. In his first letter to the Church at Corinth, Paul tells us: For no one can lay any foundation other than the one already laid, which is Jesus Christ. If any man builds on this foundation using gold, silver, costly stones, wood, hay or straw, his work will be shown for what it is, because the Day will bring it to light. It will be revealed with fire, and the fire will **test** the quality of each man's work. If what he has built survives, he will receive his reward. (1Cor 3:11-14)

The Bible never promises this life will be free from pain and suffering, in fact it emphatically states that we will **all** experience trials and tribulations in this lifetime! We must expect it. But sometimes our suffering is the result of our own poor choices, or the evil intent of others.

There are five reasons for suffering in this life:

1. Sin
   Suffering can be the result of your own sin or the sin of someone else that touches your life. Examples might be suffering divorce due to marital infidelity or crimes committed against you by others.
2. Spiritual attack
   The best example of this might be from Job. Job clearly found favor with God, he was a righteous and faithful man, but God allowed his suffering at the hand of Satan. Even Jesus suffered attack from Satan.
3. Fallen world
   We live in a fallen world since Adam and Eve were evicted from the Garden of Eden, and that event introduced disease and illnesses to the world as well, even the ground was cursed.
4. Spiritual discipline
   Suffering may come about as God chastises His people as a disciplinary measure or to get their attention. Many of the

prophets experienced this, especially Jonah, running from God.

5. Spiritual development

    Paul is a good example of God allowing suffering as he prayed for God to remove the thorn (of discipline) from him, and God refused, saying "My Grace is sufficient." Paul was to learn patience, grace and trust from God by tolerating this painful infliction, whether a physical or spiritual thorn. This prepares us for future ministry or service in the kingdom of God.

NLT 1 Peter 4:1-4 So then, since Christ suffered physical pain, you must arm yourselves with the same attitude he had, and be ready to suffer, too. For if you are willing to suffer for Christ, you have decided to stop sinning. And you won't spend the rest of your life chasing after evil desires, but you will be anxious to do the will of God. You have had enough in the past of the evil things that godless people enjoy— their immorality and lust, their feasting and drunkenness and wild parties, and their terrible worship of idols. Of course, your former friends are very surprised when you no longer join them in the wicked things they do, and they say evil things about you.

NIV 1 Peter 3:17 It is better, if it is God's will, to suffer for doing good than for doing evil.

NIV 1 Peter 4:19 So then, those who suffer according to God's will should commit themselves to their faithful Creator and continue to do good.

Further, Paul tells us: ... we know that suffering produces perseverance; perseverance, character; and character, hope. And hope does not disappoint us, because God has poured out his love into our hearts by the Holy Spirit, whom he has given us. You see, at just the right time, when we were still powerless, Christ died for the ungodly. (Romans 5:3-6)

Pain actually serves a purpose. There is a rare disease that deprives children the ability to feel pain. Most of these children do not grow up to become adults because the lack of pain causes them to do something that is fatal, like bleeding or burning to death because the absence of pain is a failure to signal when to stop before there is irreversible damage. In one case I heard of, a child rubbed her eyes so hard, the retinas were detached and she became blind. This was the first indication that the parents had that there was something wrong with their child, she could not feel any physical sensation. This is also a problem with leprosy, where the nerves are so damaged that pain cannot be felt. Indianapolis Colts Coach Tony Dungy has a son with this condition.

No one wants to experience suffering, yet Peter and Paul want us to willingly choose suffering when it is God's will for our character development. So what are God's purposes for our pain?

7 Ways God Uses Tough Times to Shape Our Lives
From the book "Finding Strength in Weakness" by William D. Black M.D.

1. Tribulation Tests Our Identity as Christians - Tribulation tests our identity. In the parable of the sower (Matt: 13:1-23), Jesus described several situations. The seed that landed on rocky places did not have much soil. It sprang up quickly, because the soil was shallow. When the sun came up, the plants were scorched, and they withered because they had no root. Jesus said that the one who received the seed that fell on rocky places is the man who hears the word and at once receives it with joy. Since he has no root, he lasts only a short time. When trouble or persecution comes because of the word, he quickly falls away. The one who received the seed that fell among thorns is the man who hears the word, but the worries of this life and the deceitfulness of wealth choke it, making it unfruitful. The seed that fell on good soil produced a good crop. By implication, that seed that fell on good soil stayed connected to the source of its life and was not destroyed by trouble, persecution, the worries of this life, or the deceitfulness of wealth. When we deal with tribulation as we should, it authenticates our true identity as believers.

2. Tribulation Tests Our Faith - These [trials] have come so that your faith - of greater worth than gold, which perishes even though refined by fire - may be proved genuine and may result in praise, glory and honor when Jesus Christ is revealed. (1 Pet. 1:7)

3. Tribulation Tests Our Sense of Purpose - When I was in my first year of medical school, I was about one minute late to histology class two or three times in a row. Our professor approached me in the laboratory and notified me that my tardiness reflected on my "sense of purpose." I was never late again, because I realized how it would reflect on my character. As it says in James, "Blessed is the man who perseveres under trial, because when he has stood the test, he will receive the crown of life that God has promised to those who love him." (James 1:2)

4. Tribulation Tests our Obedience - The reason I wrote you was to see if you would stand the test and be obedient in everything. (2 Cor. 2:9)

5. We Are Tested to Teach Us to Rely on God - We do not want you to be uninformed, brothers, about the hardships we suffered in the province of Asia. We were under great pressure, far beyond our ability to endure, so that we despaired even of life. Indeed, in our hearts we felt the sentence of death. But this happened that we might not rely on ourselves but on God, who raises the dead. He has delivered us from such a deadly peril, and he will deliver us. On him we have set our hope that he will continue to deliver us, as you help us by your prayers. Then many will give thanks on our behalf for the gracious favor granted us in answer to the prayers of many. (2 Cor. 1:8-11)

6. We Are Tested so That It will Go Well with Us - he gave you manna to eat in the desert, something your fathers had never known, to humble and to test you so that in the end it might go well with you. (Deut. 8:16)

7. Some People Do Not Pass the Test - In the New Testament, there is a Greek word, adokimos, that speaks of people who are tested but do not pass the test. It is used several times in the New Testament. I have included selected quotations. "No, I beat my body and make it my slave so that after I have preached to others, I myself will not be disqualified for the prize." (1 Cor. 9:27)

Examine yourselves to see whether you are in the faith; test yourselves. Do you not realize that Christ Jesus is in you - unless of course you fail the test? And I trust that you will discover that we have not failed the test. Now we pray to God that you will not do anything wrong. (2 Cor. 13:5-7a)

They claim to know God, but by their actions they deny him. They are detestable, disobedient and unfit for doing anything good." (Titus 1:16) "But land that produces thorns and thistles is worthless and is in danger of being cursed. In the end it will be burned. (Heb. 6:8)

Consider what 1 John 2:19 says about some who left the fellowship: "They went out from us, but they did not really belong to us. For if they had belonged to us, they would have remained with us; but their going out showed that none of them belonged to us."

As I study these concepts, I can only come to one conclusion: Salvation is a gift from God, but if your life does not show evidence of God working in it, you likely never received the gift.

10 Ways God Uses Suffering in Our Lives
From the book "Life on Hold" by Laurel Seiler Brunvoll and
David Seiler, Ph.D

1. Suffering enables you to honor God.
   Your words, actions, and attitudes paint a picture of your relationship with God. They can bring Him either honor or dishonor. They can be either a good example to others or a bad one. Do you remember what Job said when his family and all his worldly goods were suddenly gone? The Lord gave and the Lord has taken away. Blessed be the name of the Lord (Job 1:21; see also 1 Peter 1:6-7).
2. Suffering demonstrates God's power.
   It's only when you are weak—that is, not dependent upon yourself—that you can be strong in Christ. Most gladly, therefore, I will rather boast about my weakness, wrote the apostle Paul, that the power of Christ may dwell in me...for when I am weak, and then I am strong (2 Corinthians 12:9-10).
3. Suffering allows God to give His grace.
   Three times Paul asked God to remove his thorn in the flesh. God's answer was My grace is sufficient for you (2 Corinthians

12:8-9; see also 1 Corinthians 15:10; Ephesians 4:7; Philippians 2:13; 1 Peter 5:10).

4. Suffering prepares you to help others.

In 2 Corinthians 1:3-5, Paul tells the believers at Corinth that God is the God of all comfort and that they share not only His sufferings, but also His comfort. Because God will comfort you in the midst of your suffering, you will be able to comfort others with the same comfort and give them hope.

5. Suffering helps build character.

Think of one person you admire deeply. Why do think that person has such great character? Often, though not always, the people with the greatest character have experienced tragedies or walked a path of suffering. Their life experiences have shaped them into something quite beautiful. How does this happen? Paul wrote to the believers in Rome: We also exult in our tribulations, knowing that tribulation brings about perseverance; and perseverance, proven character; and, proven character hope; and hope does not disappoint, because the love of God has been poured out within our hearts through the Holy Spirit who has been given to us (Romans 5:3-5).

6. Suffering encourages you to trust God.

Children trust more easily than adults do. Too often, children grow up to be self-sufficient, independent adults who don't "need" God in their lives. Yet, Jesus reminded His disciples that the kingdom of heaven belongs to children (Matthew 19:14), and God calls us to be imitators of God, as beloved children (Ephesians 5:1). In, 2 Corinthians 1:9-10, Paul makes it very clear that he needed God and that he trusted in Him: Indeed, we had the sentence of death within ourselves in order that we should not trust in ourselves, but in God who raises the dead; who delivered us from so great a peril of death, and will deliver us, He on whom we have set our hope. And He will yet deliver us.

7. Suffering helps you learn to thank God and praise Him in everything.

First Thessalonians 5:16, 18 tells us to Rejoice always...in everything give thanks; for this is God's will for you in Christ

Jesus. Without a doubt, this is a hard task! Margaret Clarkson suggests a few ways to praise God in the midst of suffering: Praise God for Himself, His sovereignty, wisdom, never-failing mercies and compassion, love, grace, holiness, justice, and power. She recommends meditating on Scripture to help cultivate a response of praise.

8. Suffering helps you identify with Christ's suffering.
How often do you stop to think about how much Christ suffered for you? He died for you while you were still a sinner and saved you from the wrath of God (Romans 5:8-9). Read through the entire chapter of Isaiah 53 and list all the words that describe what Christ suffered for you (for example, pierced, afflicted, forsaken). How does your own suffering change your perspective on what Christ did for you? (Romans 8:17-18; Philippians 1:29, 3:10, 2 Thessalonians 1:5).

9. Suffering helps you partake of God's holiness. You have the honor and privilege of sharing in the inheritance of the saints because God the Father has qualified you (Colossians 1:12). Paul says that he does all things for the sake of the gospel so that he may become a fellow partaker of sufferings also means that we will partake of the glory that is to be revealed (1 Peter 4:12-16; 5:1). Never forget that God's precious and magnificent promises have made you a partaker of the divine nature (2 Peter 1:4).

10. Suffering offers you the chance to reflect on God's discipline.
It is possible that God has allowed this suffering in your life so that you will learn from it. Punishment is not in view here—only a divine, purposeful opportunity for growth and change. God's discipline, unlike that of an earthly parent, is perfect and will yield the peaceful fruit of righteousness so that you can share in His holiness (Hebrews 12:8-13). (Used by permission of Multnomah Publishers, Inc. Excerpt may not be reproduced without the prior written consent of Multnomah Publishers, Inc.)

Sunday, July 03, 2005 by AllAboutGOD.com

Comfort and Hope

Understanding Grief

Grief is a natural process that we experience after suffering a significant loss. While grieving is difficult and painful, it does not have to immobilize us. We can learn to be patient with ourselves and with others during periods of grief by understanding what we are going through.

What should you expect while you are coping with grief? How will you react? Do you feel tense? Remember that crying is a healthy release of tension. Keeping a "stiff upper lip" is not only difficult, but it represses your feelings, often bottling them away only to erupt at a later time and in a way you do not expect. You may also experience loss of appetite, sleeplessness, lack of concentration, and fatigue. Alcohol and drugs only mask and delay the grief process, so consider avoiding them during this time. It is also wise not to make major decisions or take on new responsibilities until your grief has subsided.

Many people experience a kaleidoscope of reactions during the process of grief. If your pain is especially intense, you may even lose interest in life itself. In order to safeguard yourself against a long period of depression as a result of grief, it is critical to discover purpose and hope outside of yourself. In time, your sense of purpose will return as the pain becomes less intense.

You may also experience guilt and find yourself asking "what if." Learning to forgive yourself and others is an important factor in overcoming this thought cycle. Anger must be expressed and shared in a healthy and appropriate manner.

When dealing with grief, increased vulnerability is inevitable. You will find that grief creates change in almost every phase of life, including social structure. Grief redefines the past-but as it passes, it can open doors to the future.

Friends and Family

It is important to know that your grief process may be uncomfortable for your friends and family. Uncertain how to ease your pain and comfort you, they often don't know what to say. If you can, let them know that it is good to talk about your loss so that they will know how you feel. If there are children around you during this time, reassure them often and express your love to them.

Practical Instruction

Consider the following ideas for managing the grief process:

- Embrace gentleness. Your body and soul need repair.
- Accept help when offered and seek help if a problem is unresolved.
- Give your body rest. When possible, go to bed earlier.
- Get together with friends and meet new people. Focusing on others will help you deal with the pain. Holidays and special occasions are difficult, so lean on your family and friends for support.
- Be patient. If you feel depressed for awhile, it is okay.
- Look for comforting activities. Learn to express your feelings, talk, write, sing, exercise, and cry. Learn more about grief recovery; a greater understanding helps us cope.
- Good nutrition is important. Avoid junk food.

NIV James 1:2-4 Consider it pure joy, my brothers, whenever you face trials of many kinds, because you know that the testing of your faith develops perseverance. Perseverance must finish its work so that you may be mature and complete, not lacking anything.

Redemption means nothing to the person who sees no need to be redeemed. If we don't recognize our own sin, our deviation from God's perfect holiness, we won't see any need to be forgiven. To sin is to "miss the mark" of perfection, and we can only enter the kingdom of God in the afterlife if we are perfect and holy. Since we all miss that mark, we have only one way to enter the kingdom of God, which is through the One who can cleanse us and make us holy, the One who has paid for our redemption by His suffering, death and conquering death. That is Jesus, the Jewish Messiah, Savior of all mankind, to all who will turn to Him, He will guarantee your eternal joy with no pain or suffering, no tears or hunger, no thirst or disability. We all want life to be free from pain and suffering, and only Jesus guarantees He will make it so, in His perfect timing, and all of our current sufferings will pass like the morning mist.

So our response to pain and suffering should be to always trust in God, to empathize with others and reach out to people who are experiencing similar circumstances. We can love them, comfort them and give them hope that these hardships are always temporary and there is healing and hope through Jesus Christ who suffered and died for us, then conquered both. He appeared to hundreds of people and proved to us that He is the way; that we must follow Him and Him alone if we desire eternal fellowship free from pain, suffering and death. After taking his daughter to the pediatrician for shots, and observing her reaction to what she knew was coming, Kyle Idleman put it this way, "When suffering comes, hang onto God and don't let go."

Habakkuk 3:17-19 Though the fig tree does not bud and there are no grapes on the vines, though the olive crop fails and the fields produce no food, though there are no sheep in the pen and no cattle in the stalls, yet I will rejoice in the LORD, I will be joyful in God my Savior. The Sovereign LORD is my strength…

Revelation 21:4-5 He will wipe every tear from their eyes. There will be no more death or mourning or crying or pain, for the old order of things has passed away." He who was seated on the throne said, "I am making everything new!"

No other religion makes that claim or offers such hope. I do not care to achieve nirvana, I don't want to be reincarnated as a cow or a gnat, seventy virgins would only last about seventy nights (eternity is much longer) and atheism makes it all meaningless. Most people believe in an afterlife. Only Jesus tells us what that life will be like, depending on our attitude toward Him and the choices we make in THIS life.

If you are struggling with depression or anxiety issues, "Healing Is a Choice" by Steve Arterburn may be helpful in lifting those burdens that lead to depression and anxiety. It is a book and an intensive workshop. Find out more at www.healingisachoice.com

Resources:

"God Will Make A Way – What To Do When You Don't Know What To Do" by Drs. Henry Cloud and John Townsend © 2002 Integrity Publishers, 5250 Virginia Way, Suite 110, Brentwood, TN 37027

"Changes that Heal –How to Understand Your Past to Ensure a Healthier Future" by Dr. Henry Cloud © 1990, 1992 Zondervan Publishing House, Grand Rapids, MI 49530

"Secrets of the Vine – Breaking Through to Abundance" by Bruce Wilkerson © 2006 Multnomah Publishers, 601 N. Larch Street, Sisters, OR 97759

"Job: A Man of Heroic Endurance" by Charles R. Swindoll © 2004 W Publishing Group, P.O.Box 141000, Nashville, TN 37214

"Healing is a Choice – Ten Decisions That Will Transform Your Life & Ten Lies That Can Prevent You From Making Them" by Stephen Arterburn © 2005 Thomas Nelson Publishers, Nashville, TN

"Questions I Have About Suffering" Kyle Idleman audio sermon
LW2838   www.livingword.org

Websites:

Southeast Christian Church, Louisville, KY www.southeastchristian. org

Soulcare   http://soulcare.southeastchristian.org

Depression and Anxiety   www.healingisachoice.com

New Life Ministries – Stephen Arterburn www.newlife.com

Focus on the Family   www.troubledwith.com

Drs. Henry Cloud and John Townsend www.cloudtownsend.com

Chapter 9 – Loss of a family member or friend

Death and dying can be a very difficult subject. It is often only discussed when there has been a loss, as people are just beginning the grieving process. As we process our grief, we go through five stages which include denial and isolation, anger, bargaining, depression and acceptance.

One of the lies that has been perpetuated in our society is that time heals all wounds. It doesn't. In fact, it usually does just the opposite. As we bury our hurts, time tends to cause our wounds to fester and get worse, the pain causes our problems to multiply and take on a variety of other facades that protect us from our hurts. This is what makes it difficult for us to determine exactly where our problems lie, and why therapy with a good, experienced counselor can help you sort through the symptoms to get at the root of the problem. Healing our deep wounds requires facing the hurt, grieving that which was lost, and getting into a healing community of safe people. We have to make the choice to face the hurts or they will never go away. It seems like it is easier to hide them and publicly try to convince our friends and family we are fine, but the reality is we must take the three-year-old approach. Get a big Band-Aid with a colorful cartoon character on it and show everyone you love where the hurt is! Don't bury the emotions, but feel them, process them and be healed in the presence of those who love you.

From: allaboutlifechallenges.org

Dealing with Death - Experienced By Everyone

Dealing with death is a life experience that no one wants to face. Life can often seem like swimming in the ocean during high tide. Even if we know how to swim and jump over the big waves at just the right time, when we least expect it-wham! We are broadsided, and find ourselves spinning and bouncing off the bottom of the ocean with a mouth full of sand. If we fight, it takes longer to get to the surface. But if we float with the current, we come right to the top. Floating when we are frightened is difficult. It takes trust and concentration. Dealing with the death of a loved one is similar. In order to cope, it takes trust.

Death is nearly always accompanied by questions - especially "why." Whether we are facing our own death, or the death of someone we love, we want answers. *Why is this happening? What did I do to deserve this? Is there life after death?* The sooner we learn to float - to trust - the easier it is to discover the answers we are seeking.

Dealing with Death - The True Position

When dealing with death, the solution is the same whether the death is our own or that of a loved one. As hard as it is to accept, we must understand that death is a part of life. As some have quipped, death is the only thing in life that comes with a 100% guarantee.

It is helpful to realize that while our bodies are mortal, all human beings are eternal - our soul and spirit will never die. Our spirits - the essence of who we are - will live forever!

Dealing with Death - No greater Love

Dealing with death was not a problem for Adam and Eve-the first man and woman who ever lived. However, once they sinned against God, things changed. Dying was a result of Adam's sin of disobedience.

We may think of death as final, but there is no end in the plan of God. We are eternal beings in His sight. Have you ever wondered why, even though your body might be aging, you don't feel "older" inside? It's because your spirit is eternal. The Bible says that God has placed eternity in our hearts (Ecclesiastes 3:11).

God desires for us to spend eternity with Him, yet He has left that choice up to us. God has made all the provisions for us to be with Him forever. He has no greater love than His love for us.

Dealing with Death - What is the issue?
Dealing with death is largely influenced by what we think of Jesus Christ. It also affects where we will spend eternity. In His infinite love, God sent His Son Jesus to die for us. When we believe in Jesus Christ and that He died as payment for our sins, we are guaranteed eternal life with Him forever.

If you are a child of God, dying is a promotion. Do we want to be with God forever? Do we understand that the only other option is to be separated from Him forever? Jesus said, "...I am the resurrection and the life. He who believes in me will live, even though he dies; and whoever lives and believes in me will never die. Do you believe this?" (John 11:25-26).

How we respond to the gift of Jesus Christ will determine where we spend eternity. God the Father loves all His creation and He waits on high to bless and redeem us. Psalm 116:15 says, "Precious in the sight of the LORD is the death of his saints." If we know Christ as our personal Savior, we need not fear dying. As for those we love, it becomes our responsibility as believers to pray for the salvation of those who do not know Him. For those who do, death is a celebration - a homecoming!

As we begin to think of ourselves as eternal beings, the realization that there is a future will help us cope with the present circumstances. We begin to ask specific questions concerning eternity. Will we be separated from our earthly body and separated from loved ones? Will we see them again? How do we define separation? How do we deal with separation in life and in death? God has a plan for us here on earth. God has a plan for eternity - He reveals it to us.

What about you? Do you know Christ as your Savior today? If you have not yet made that decision, why not do it now.

For the Christian, death is not the worst that can happen to a person. It is tragic, and no one wishes to face it, but it is inevitable for most. Many parents who have lost a child have found comfort in knowing they will one day be reunited with their child in heaven.

Jesus mourned with those saddened by the deaths of loved ones, sharing the grief of their loss even knowing he would raise them from the dead, because he had such great compassion for what people were going through. It is the resurrection from death that is our hope for the future, the promise only Christians have, guaranteed by Jesus himself, who overcame death and is alive today.

But what if you are not a Christian? I'll let my friend Dr. David Reagan answer the question:

"What Happens When You Die?" (By Dr. David Reagan)

If several years ago you had asked me what happens when you die, I would have given you a pathetic answer. I would have told you that when you die your soul goes to sleep until the Lord returns. At the return of the Lord, your soul is resurrected and judged, and you are either consigned to Hell or allowed to enter Heaven. My conception of Heaven was that of a spirit world where the saved spend eternity as disembodied spirits, floating around on clouds, playing harps.

A Mistaken View

Needless to say, I couldn't get very excited about all that. I sure didn't like the idea of being unconscious in the grave for eons of time. Nor could I develop any enthusiasm for the prospect of being a disembodied spirit with no particular identity or personality. And the idea of playing a harp for all eternity was downright scandalous, for I had been taught that instrumental music in worship was an abomination! You can imagine, therefore, the sense of shock I felt when I started studying Bible prophecy and discovered that all these ideas of mine about life after death were foreign to God's Word. But my shock quickly gave way to exhilaration when I discovered what the Lord really has in store for me.

The Biblical View

I learned from God's Word that when those of us who are Christians die, our spirits never lose their consciousness (Phils.

1:23). Instead, our fully conscious spirits are immediately ushered into the presence of Jesus by His holy angels (2 Cor. 5:8). Our spirits remain in the Lord's presence until He appears for His Church. At that time, He brings our spirits with Him, resurrects our bodies, reunites our spirits with our bodies, and then glorifies our bodies, perfecting them and rendering them eternal (1 Thess 4:13-18). We return with Him to Heaven in our glorified bodies where we are judged for our works to determine our degrees of rewards (2 Cor. 5:10). When this judgment is completed, we participate in a glorious wedding feast to celebrate the union of Jesus and His Bride, the Church (Rev. 19:7-9).

Witnesses of Glory

At the conclusion of the feast, we burst from the heavens with Jesus, returning with Him to the earth in glory (Rev. 19:14). We witness His victory at Armageddon, we shout "Hallelujah!" as He is crowned King of kings and Lord of lords, and we revel in His glory as He begins to reign over all the earth from Mt. Zion in Jerusalem (Zech. 14:1-9;

Rev. 19:17-21). For a thousand years we participate in that reign, assisting Him with the instruction, administration, and enforcement of His perfect laws (Rev. 20:1-6). We see the earth regenerated and nature reconciled (Isa. 11:6-9). We see holiness abound and the earth flooded with peace, righteousness and justice (Micah 4:1-7). At the end of the Millennium we witness the release of Satan to deceive the nations. We see the truly despicable nature of the heart of Man as millions rally to Satan in his attempt to overthrow the throne of Jesus. But we will shout "Hallelujah!" again when we witness God's supernatural destruction of Satan's armies and see Satan himself cast into Hell where he will be tormented forever (Rev. 20:7-10). We will next witness the Great White Throne Judgment when the unrighteous are resurrected to stand before God. We will see perfect holiness and justice in action as God pronounces His terrible judgment upon this congregation of the damned who have rejected His gift of love and mercy in Jesus Christ (Rev. 20:11-13). Jesus will be fully vindicated as every knee shall bow and every tongue confesses that He is Lord. Then the unrighteous will receive their just reward as they are cast into Hell (Rev. 20:14-15).

Witnesses of a New Creation

We will then witness the most spectacular fireworks display in all of history. We will be taken to the New Jerusalem, the eternal mansion prepared by Jesus for His Bride, and from there we will watch as God renovates this earth with fire, burning away all the filth and pollution left by Satan's last battle (2 Peter 3:12-13). Just as the angels rejoiced when God created the universe, we will rejoice as we watch God superheat this earth and reshape it like a hot ball of wax into the New Earth, the eternal earth, the paradise where we will live forever in the presence of God (Rev. 21:1). What a glorious moment it will be when we are lowered to the New Earth inside the fabulous New Jerusalem (Rev. 21:2). God will come down from Heaven to dwell with us (Rev. 21:3). He will proclaim "Behold, I make all things new" (Rev. 21:5) We will see God face to face (Rev. 22:4). He will wipe away all our tears (Rev. 21:4). Death will be no more (Rev. 21:4). We will be given new names (Rev. 2:17), and we will exist as individual personalities encased in perfect bodies (Phils. 3:21). And we will grow eternally in knowledge and love of our infinite Creator, honoring Him with our talents and gifts. Now, I can get excited about that!

The Word vs. Tradition

Isn't it amazing how far we can drift away from the Word of God when we stop reading His Word and start mouthing the traditions of men? As I kept making one discovery after another in God's Prophetic Word that ran contrary to what I had been taught, I began to wonder about the origin of the doctrines I had learned. It didn't take me long to discover that the source was Greek philosophy. The first attempt to mix the concepts of Greek philosophy with the teachings of God's Word came very early in the history of the Church. The attempt was called Gnosticism. The Gnostic heresy arose among the first Gentile converts because they tried to Hellenize the Scriptures; that is, they tried to make the Scriptures conform to the basic tenets of Greek philosophy. The Greeks believed that the material universe, including the human body, was evil. This negative view of the creation was diametrically opposed to Hebrew thought, as revealed in the Bible. To the Hebrew mind, the world was created good (Genesis 1:31). And even though the goodness of the creation was corrupted by the sin of Man (Isaiah 24:5-6), the creation still reflects to some degree the glory of God (Psalms 19:1). Most important, the creation will someday be redeemed by God (Romans 8:18-23).

The Gnostic Heresy

When the first Gentiles were converted to the Gospel, their Greek-mind set immediately collided with some of the fundamental teachings of Christianity. For example, they wondered, "How could Jesus have come in the flesh if He was God? God is holy. How can He who is holy be encased in a body which is evil?" In short, because they viewed the material universe as evil, they could not accept the Bible's teaching that God became incarnate in the flesh. Their response was to develop the Gnostic heresy that Jesus was a spirit being or phantom who never took on the flesh and therefore never experienced physical death. This heresy is denounced strongly in Scripture. In 1 John 4:1-2 we are told to test those who seek our spiritual fellowship by asking them to confess "that Jesus Christ has come in the flesh."

The Augustinian Corruption

About 400 A.D. a remarkable theologian by the name of St. Augustine attempted to Hellenize what the Scriptures taught about end time events and life after death. Augustine was very successful in his attempt. His views were adopted by the Council of Ephesus in 431 A.D. and have remained Catholic dogma to this day. The influence of Greek philosophy would not allow Augustine to accept what the Bible taught about life after death. For example, the Bible says the saints will spend eternity in glorified bodies on a New Earth

(Revelation 21:1-7). Such a concept was anathema to the Greek mind of Augustine. If the material world is evil, then he reasoned that the material world must cease to exist when the Lord returns. Augustine solved the problem by spiritualizing what the Bible said. He did this by arguing that the "new earth" of Revelation 21 is just symbolic language for Heaven. Most professing Christians today, both Catholic and Protestant hold Augustine's views. That means that most of Christianity today teaches Greek philosophy rather than the Word of God when it comes to the realm of end time prophecy and life after death.

The Intermediate State

Some of the greatest confusion about life after death relates to the intermediate state between death and eternity. Some people advocate a concept called "soul sleep." They argue that both the saved and unsaved are unconscious after death until the return of Jesus. But the Bible makes it crystal clear that our spirit does not lose its consciousness at death. The only thing that "falls asleep" is our body — in a symbolic sense. Paul says in 2 Corinthians 5:8 that he would prefer to be "absent from the body and at home with the Lord." In Philippians 1:21 he observes, "For me to live is Christ and to die is gain." He then adds in verse 23 that his desire is "to depart and be with Christ." Paul certainly did not expect to be in a coma after he died! If then our spirits retain their consciousness after death, where do they go? The Bible teaches that prior to the resurrection of Jesus, the spirits of the dead went to a place called Hades ("Sheol" in the Old Testament). The spirits existed there consciously in one of two compartments, either Paradise or Torments. This concept is pictured graphically in Jesus' story of the rich man and Lazarus (Luke 16:19-31). The Bible indicates that after the death of Jesus on the Cross, He descended into Hades and declared to all the spirits there His triumph over Satan (1 Peter 3:18-19; 4:6). The Bible also indicates that after His resurrection, when He ascended into Heaven, Jesus took Paradise with Him, transferring the spirits of dead saints from Hades to Heaven (Ephesians 4:8-9 and 2 Corinthians 12:1-4). The spirits of dead saints are thereafter pictured as being in Heaven before the throne of God (See Revelation 6:9 and 7:9). The spirits of the righteous dead could not go directly to Heaven before the Cross because their sins were not forgiven. Instead, their sins were merely covered by their faith. The forgiveness of their sins had to await the shedding of the blood of Christ (Leviticus 17:11; Romans 5:8-9; Hebrews 9:22).

Events at Death

So, what happens when you die? If you are a child of God, your spirit is immediately ushered into the bosom of Jesus by His holy angels. Your spirit remains in Heaven, in the presence of God, until the time of the Rapture. When Jesus comes for His Church, He brings your spirit with Him, resurrects and glorifies your body, making it eternal in nature (1 Corinthians 15 and 1 Thessalonians 4). You reign with Christ for a thousand years and then live eternally with Him on the new earth (Revelation 20-22). If you are not a child of God, then your spirit goes to Hades at your death. This is a place of torments where your spirit is held until the resurrection of the unrighteous, which takes place at the end of the millennial reign of Jesus. At that resurrection you are taken before the Great White Throne of God where you are judged by your works and then condemned to the "second death," which is the "lake of fire" or Hell (Revelation 20:11-15).

Preparing for Eternity

One thing is certain: "Every knee shall bow and every tongue confess that 'Jesus is Lord!'" (Isaiah 45:23; Romans 14:11). Your eternal destiny will be determined by *when* you make this confession. If it is made before you die, then you will spend eternity with God. If not, then you will make the confession at the Great White Throne judgment before you are cast into Hell. To spend eternity with God, your confession of Jesus as Lord must be made *now.*

*"If you confess with your mouth Jesus as Lord, and believe
in your heart that God raised Him from the dead, you shall
be saved"* — Romans 10:9

There is Hope and a Future

The grief process at the onset is difficult, but as time passes we'll begin again to look for reasons to hope. Hope based on absolutes and an eternal future offers a comforting and motivating perspective. In the Psalms we are told, "I would have lost heart, unless I had believed that I would see the goodness of the LORD in the land of the living."

God promises us refreshment and hope, first through salvation in the Lord Jesus Christ, who died for our sins and rose again to give us all a future in heaven. **If we believe in Jesus Christ**, we not only have a future here on earth but **we have a future** in heaven with Him. John 3:36a says, "He who believes in the Son has everlasting life; and he who does not believe the Son shall not see life."

When we believe in Jesus Christ, grief soon turns to hope. Before long, we are greeting each day again with anticipation and eagerly awaiting our future with Him. John 10:28 says, "And I give them eternal life, and they shall never perish; nor shall anyone snatch them out of My hand."

Do you believe this? Then you do not sorrow (grieve) as those who have no hope (1 Thessalonians 4:13b).

10 Tips for Healthy Grieving by Stephen Arterburn

1. Stay "connected" with someone. Find a trusted friend, pastor or counselor with whom you can be real. Speak what's on your mind and in your heart. If this feels one-sided, let that be okay for this period of your life. Chances are the other person will find meaning in what they're doing. And the time will come when you'll have the chance to be a good listener for someone else. You'll be a better listener then if you're a good talker now.

2. Don't be afraid to tell people what helps you and what doesn't. People around you may not understand what you need - so tell them. If you need more time alone, or assistance with chores

you're unable to complete, or an occasional hug, be honest. People can't read your mind, so you'll have to speak it.

3. Invite someone to be your telephone buddy. If your grief and sadness hit you especially hard at times and you have no one nearby to turn to, ask someone you trust to be your telephone buddy. Ask their permission for you to call them whenever you feel you're in trouble, day or night. Then put their number beside your phone and call them if you need them.

4. Journal. Write out your thoughts, feelings and prayers. Be as honest as you can. In time, go back through your writings and notice how you're changing and growing. Write about that, too.

5. Write the person who died. Write a letter to your loved one, thoughts you wish you could express if they were present. This can be a key step in coming to terms with your feelings and bringing a degree of healing closure.

6. Consider a church or community grief support group. You were not created to be alone all the time. Gathering with others who've experienced similar loss can remove the isolation so often associated with grief.

7. Plant something living as a memorial. Plant a flower, a bush or a tree in memory of the one who died. Or plant several things. Do this ceremonially if you wish, perhaps with others present. If you do this planting where you live, you can watch it grow and change day by day, season by season. You can even make it a part of special times of remembrance in the future.

8. Give yourself permission to change some things. As soon as it seems right, alter some things in your home to make clear this significant change that has occurred. Rearrange a room or replace a piece of furniture or give away certain items that will never again be used. This doesn't mean to remove all signs of the one who died. But, preserving a "shrine" to your lost loved one can be harmful, in that it may not allow for the closure process to begin.

9. Allow yourself to laugh and cry. Sometimes something funny will happen to you, just like it used to. When that happens, go ahead and laugh if it feels funny to you. You won't be dese-

crating your loved one's memory. Crying goes naturally with grief. Tears well up and fall even when you least expect them. It may feel awkward to you, but this is not unusual for a person in your situation. A good rule of thumb is this: if you feel like crying, then cry.

10. Do something to help someone else. Step out of your own problems from time to time and devote your attention to someone else. Offer a gift or your service. Placing your focus on someone else will help you avoid the traps of self-pity and anger.[r]

Resources:

"Safe in the Arms of God – Truth From Heaven About the Death of a Child" by John MacArthur © 2003 Thomas Nelson Publishers, Nashville, TN

"Grieving the Loss of Someone You Love – Daily Meditations to Help You Through the Grieving Process" by Raymond R. Mitsch & Lynn Brookside © 1993 Regal Books by Gospel Light, Ventura, CA

"Where is God When It Hurts? A Comforting, Healing Guide for Coping with Hard Times" by Philip Yancey © 1977, 1990, 2002 Zondervan, Grand Rapids, MI 49530 – Gold Medallion Book Award Winner

"Holding on to your faith even **When God Doesn't Make Sense"** by Dr. James Dobson © 1993, 1997 Tyndale House Publishers, Wheaton, IL - 1994 Gold Medallion Winner

"Healing is a Choice – Ten Decisions That Will Transform Your Life & Ten Lies That Can Prevent You From Making Them" by Stephen Arterburn © 2005 Thomas Nelson Publishers, Nashville, TN

"Grieving the Loss of a Loved One" A Devotional Companion by Kathe Wunnenberg © 2000 Zondervan, Grand Rapids, MI 49530

www.newlife.com   audio CD: Processing Grief Stephen Arterburn & Jill Hubbard

Websites:
www.gty.org   Grace to You Ministries with John MacArthur

www.healingisachoice.com	Healing is a Choice workshops, weekend seminars
www.lamblion.com	Lamb and Lion Ministries of Dr. David Reagan
www.allaboutlifechallenges.org	Resources for everyone
www.family.org	Focus on the Family with Dr. James Dobson
http://troubledwith.com/	Focus on the Family helpsite
www.southeastchristian.org	Church in Louisville, KY with resources for everyone
www.livingword.org	Southeast Christian Church online media center

Chapter 10 – Financial Issues

Financial issues are one of the leading causes of dissension in adult relationships. Too often, we value our "stuff" more than we value the relationship. Occasionally, we experience an event like the 9-11 attacks, or hurricane Katrina, and we get a perspective on the importance of "stuff" that we all too often need a refresher on. That's when we see what our priorities SHOULD be: Faith in God, the safety of our family and friends, water, food, clothing, shelter, medical attention and employment. Everything else is gravy. Statistics show that money matters are a contributing factor for 57 - 70% of divorces in the U.S.

Most of us are familiar with these truisms, but we seldom heed them:

- The borrower is servant to the lender.
- If your outflow is more than your income, your upkeep will be your downfall.
- DEBT- Don't Even Buy That!
- Give to God what is right, not what is left.

And who among us has never experienced "buyers' remorse"? When we realize we probably didn't need that widget as much as we thought. When the pleasure of the purchase lasts only until the pain of the payment. American advertising DEPENDS on our impulses to buy what we don't really need and usually can't afford.

I have come to believe in the 80-10-10 principle, which says simply, you should live on 80% of your take-home pay, give 10% to God and pay yourself 10% for your own savings. As your income grows, these percentages ensure real dollar increases in each area as well, and you should never have any money problems, barring a catastrophe. If catastrophe does strike, you will have reserves to get you through. If you follow this simple principle, you will be ahead of most "normal" people, since most "normal" people in the U.S. are broke, living paycheck to paycheck and have more debt than they are comfortable with. In 2005, the average household had over $8,000 in credit card debt. That's not much on a six figure income. It's a huge amount when you are just starting out, living on social security, or your income is nearer the poverty level of $19,350 (HHS) for a family of four. It is still a substantial burden for the average household income of $41,000-$48,000 (2005 Census Report).

How did we get into this situation? It's all about our attitude toward money and our attitude toward others. I know it's hard to save money when your neighbor keeps buying things you can't afford. But, if you want to live like nobody else, you have to look at your finances like nobody else. If you want to be "normal", you will be broke and in debt all of your life.

There are three ways we go about mishandling our money: Hoarding, controlling and irresponsible spending.

Hoarding is gathering all you can and hiding or storing it out of gluttony, even when you have more than enough. This is condemned in the Bible in the parable of the talents, where the servant who was given only one talent buried it instead of investing it. That servant was referred to as wicked, and his talent was given to the servant who had invested five talents and doubled them to ten. God wants us to give back a tithe, to give as we have been blessed, or all of our wealth will dry up. When we give to the needy, our blessings increase.

Controlling is not spending it when it is needed, being too miserly. If Joseph had not opened the storehouses in Egypt when the famine had started, all that had been saved for that purpose would not have been available to the people who desperately needed it, and they would have perished while sufficient food supplies went untouched. That would have been irresponsible and evil.

Good stewardship requires discipline in saving, investing and purchasing. Everything belongs to God. We can't take it with us when we depart. Job said: NIV Job 1:21 ..."Naked I came from my mother's womb, and naked I will depart. The LORD gave and the LORD has taken away; may the name of the LORD be praised." Most of us don't have problems with hoarding money, but if you do, that is a stumbling block to the kingdom of God. You need to learn to be generous, sharing your wealth and your wisdom with the younger and less educated among us.

Spending irresponsibly is simply buying things indiscriminately. Look for good deals, don't pay more for goods or services than is necessary and reasonable. Don't buy useless junk and don't spend money you don't have! Help your children decide what is worthwhile to spend their money on. Responsible spending is being a good steward of all that we have been trusted with. To avoid irresponsible spending, I recommend these steps to adult financial responsibility, in priority order:

1. Establish an emergency fund.

You should have at least $1,000, to cover any immediate need for car repairs, travel for a funeral or sudden family disability, appliance repairs or replacement (it's hard to live today without a refrigerator or clothes dryer). If you are married, discuss with your spouse what level this fund should be at, it might be $5,000 or $10,000, depending on your income and joint comfort level. REMEMBER: this fund is ONLY to be used for true, unexpected emergencies. If your car or appliances are old and you know they will be needing repairs more often, these should be budgeted for repair or replacement before they die. With this emergency fund, you will not have to put these occurrences on a credit card at obscene interest rates; you will have the emergency cash available if a need arises. Men: set up this emergency fund and LEAVE IT ALONE! You will be surprised at how it will change the way your wife treats you, especially if she is the saver and you are the spender. Compromise in marriage isn't letting her buy a new wardrobe because she let you get those new golf clubs if the MasterCard bill hasn't been paid off in five years.

2. Set up a budget.

Sit down with pencil, paper, calculator, checkbook and all monthly bills and determine how much is being spent each month and where the money is going. Generally, if you spend more than 70% on housing, food and transportation combined, you will have trouble staying within a balanced budget. Hopefully, the income exceeds the required payments. The excess then goes into the emergency fund first. When that is built up, the excess goes into a money market or savings account where you will accrue a minimum of one to three months of these budgeted expenses. Again, discuss with your spouse what your comfort level is, for some it is one month, for others it may be as much as six months. This fund is to be used in the event of a loss of income. If you lose your job, get demoted, commissions drop off, go on strike or have an extended illness, a temporary loss of income will not be an immediate disaster. You have bought yourself one to six months of time to get well, find a new job and get your income back up to where it was without getting behind in your payments. It also buys time if the future looks bleak, to come up with a new plan and to reduce household spending. Revisit your budget at least annually. Make adjustments for inflation, rising fuel costs, increased income, paid off debts, holiday spending or other changes to monthly cash flow.

3. Reduce your debt, with a goal to eliminate ALL debt.

If you are faced with lost income, or your income is currently less than your outflow, you have a problem. You have to reduce your bills. Let me start with the obvious. If you have toys you don't need and can't afford, get rid of them. Airplanes, motor homes, boats, campers, extra cars or motorcycles are all luxury items. Sell them and pay off those debts. If you have credit card debts, stop using the cards immediately! If you can transfer a balance to a card with a *permanently* lower rate, that will lower your minimum monthly payment. You should be able to call your credit card companies and negotiate a lower *permanent* interest rate. Most will lower an 18%

or higher rate to 9-14%, if you have excellent credit and no late payments, you should be able to get even as low as 5-9%. If that is not possible, and you have equity in your home, you may be able to get a fixed rate second mortgage, currently around 6-7% with good credit. That will lower your interest rate, and the interest should be tax deductible on the home equity loan. Do this ONLY if you can pay off the credit card and never use it again. Put it in a safe deposit box at the bank where you don't have easy access to it, or simply close the account and cut up the card. Do not apply for new credit cards. If you fail to do this, you will run the credit card balance back up to where it was (maxed out) AND have the second mortgage besides! You will be worse off than before. Avoid a home equity line of credit (HELOC), as these are usually variable rate loans amortized over 15 years and you are paying INTEREST ONLY with the remainder of the loan due at the end of the term if you only make the minimum payments. You never get rid of the debt, and that is my goal here, to put you on a course of action that will eliminate your debt, not just put it off to a later date.

If you still need to cut costs, you will have to cut back on life-style items. Your basic needs are medicine, water, food, clothing, shelter, basic utilities, transportation, insurance and work. Now you have some tough choices to make. You may need to sell your home and buy a cheaper one, or rent until you can afford to buy a home. You do not need cable or satellite TV at $40+/mo ($480/yr). If you have fairly new items that you can sell to eliminate the debt, do it. You may have to sell your late model car to get rid of that payment, and buy a car or motorcycle that is economical, reliable and ten years old. You may not even need a car. Try public transportation or riding a bike, or find someone you can commute with. You do not need a cell phone at $35+/mo ($420/yr). You do not need magazine subscriptions. You don't even need a newspaper. Ask a neighbor for their unused coupon section, most of them aren't clipping coupons anyway. Yes, you may have to lose your pride, you are broke and you are trying to fix that! If you have to have internet service, go back to dial-up for 9.95 a month. You don't have to pay $50 a month for high speed access ($600/yr). Use the local library for that. Cut down on impulse spending on lattes and junk food snacks. Put all of these savings toward paying off your debts. Find a good church in your area that has a ministry that helps people with financial responsibility and attend services there every week.

There are two schools of thought on debt elimination. Simple math tells us to pay off our highest interest rate debts first, paying off that 18% credit card before that 4% card. **IF** you have the discipline to do that, that is the fastest way out of debt. However, human nature is basically an impatient nature; we live in a fast-food society and we want results immediately. For this reason, Dave Ramsey recommends paying off your *lowest balance* credit card first, even if it has a lower interest rate; then the next lowest balance and so on. In this way, we feel like we are accomplishing something when we see that first balance dropping, then eliminated; and we are motivated by this sense of progress to keep hacking away at it. For most of us, this is probably the better method of debt reduction, so we can see small victories early on and be motivated to redouble our efforts toward total debt elimination.

I recommend eliminating debts in the following order:

1. Credit cards and unsecured debts first (like HELOCs, signature loans at 24%, etc.)
2. Automobile loans (usually secured by the vehicle)
3. Second mortgages (secured by the equity in your home)
4. Student loans (usually low payments and low interest rates, unsecured)
5. Primary mortgages – which should be 15 year fixed rate

I don't recommend an interest only mortgage, that's just putting off the inevitable fact that you got a loan on a house you can't afford. Buy less house. Yes, you might have to leave California to do that. I don't recommend variable rate loans *right now* (2005) because interest rates are rising and likely will continue to rise for the foreseeable future. A variable rate loan is only advisable in an economy with *falling* interest rates, because eventually you will have to lock in the rate or refinance the loan, and you can lock in at a lower rate. Refinancing is fine in a falling rate economy also; it will cost you more however, in a *rising rate* economy like we have right now. I also do not recommend a 30 year mortgage if you can avoid it, just because the length of the loan increases the total interest dramatically! Look at the difference on a $150,000 loan:

150,000 / 30 years at 6% - payment of $900/mo P&I Total cost $150,000 + $370,000 interest = $520,000
150,000 / 15 years at 5.5% - payment of $1225/mo P&I Total cost $150,000 + $123,750 interest = $273,750

Typically, you can get a 15 year rate half a point lower than a 30 year rate. The above numbers are currently available (2005) from most reputable mortgage lenders. In our example above, it will cost $246,250 more for the same house. That's $246,250 more for retirement, college, travel, to start a business, give to charity or whatever you want. That's $246,250 you didn't give to the lender for the same house. And your home is completely paid for in just 15 years! As interest rates rise, these numbers become more dramatic. The borrower truly is slave to the lender. What if you can't swing $1225 a month, but you can do $1100 a month? You can get a 30 year mortgage, and pay the additional $200 a month toward the *principal* on that loan, which will substantially reduce the total interest paid, as well as knocking years off of the term. You may even be able to refinance later at a more favorable 15 year fixed rate as your income level rises and you can afford the $1225 payment. Anything you can do to lower the interest rate and reduce the term of the loan will be money in YOUR bank account, instead of someone else's profit. If you move around a lot, you are probably better off renting instead of purchasing, unless your employer handles the sale and purchase of your home or guarantees the price.

If you need professional financial advice, seek a good financial counselor who can help with your specific financial situation. There are also professional debt management companies who will help you renegotiate your debts. Filing bankruptcy is bad for your credit and your reputation, and should only be a last resort. Using a debt reduction plan to get creditors to write off some of your debts is less detrimental than bankruptcy, but only slightly less. That would be the second to last resort to consider. The bottom line is, if you incurred the debt, you owe the money and you should make every honest effort to repay your obligations to the best of your ability. That's what lenders expect, that's what God expects, and that's what keeps your good reputation intact. NLT Proverbs 22:1 Choose a good reputation over great riches, for being held in high esteem is better than having silver or gold.

4. Increase your income.

You can increase your income in several ways. If you get a tax refund every year, increase the number of dependents you are claiming to have less tax withheld from your paycheck. Use the worksheet that comes with the W-4 withholding form. You can claim 0-9 dependents with this form. If you owe money to the IRS each year, you need to increase the amount withheld. The idea is to break even. You don't want to owe the IRS money, and you don't want to give the IRS an interest free loan with your money. You can't afford it.

If you are contributing to a Roth IRA or 401k, stop it; especially if your employer does not match your contributions. You need to concentrate on eliminating debt right now, you don't have extra for retirement at this time. Do not contribute more than your employer matches until you have your debts under control.

Work overtime if it is available. This can be a strain on a marriage, but so is financial stress. Talk to your spouse about it. Share your plan for eliminating debt, figure out how long it will take to get things under control, and agree to work the overtime ONLY until that goal is reached and you both can sleep easier. You might need to take a second job delivering pizzas or smashing boxes for a package delivery company, they always need help. There are always temporary jobs available in retail during the Christmas gift giving season. Your spouse may agree to work overtime or get a second job. These should be seen as short term solutions, only until the debts are manageable on your regular income, 80% of your normal take-home pay. The long term solution is to live within your means, select a job with a promotional future for increasing your income, or get some more education to find a better job or start your own business.

5. Plan for retirement.

Now that your debts are under control and you are living within your means, you have your emergency fund and a few months worth of bills saved up; you find you have some money left over at the end of the month. Give to your church. Increase your giving until you are giving 10%, and you are at the 80-10-10 stage of cash flow. Now you can contribute to that 401k or Roth IRA, but only the excess amount. As your income increases, you can increase these contributions to about 15%. Once they are maxed out (by federal limits), you can contribute after-tax dollars, or begin investing your dollars for additional retirement income, college expenses and charitable contributions. You can accelerate the payoff of your home. As your car(s) and home are paid off, you will be able to live on far less than 80%. Now you can enjoy vacations and extravagances without incurring debt! You are living like nobody else because you don't have debt like everybody else!

Now you are ready to work on investing for college, retirement and estate planning. I recommend professional financial advisors and getting as much knowledge as you need before risking any money in areas you are not familiar with. Most of what I have learned, I found through David and Tom Gardner at The Motley Fool website, www.fool.com. Between their website and their books and subscription services, they provide an incredible wealth of information to the individual investor, whether just beginning at Fool's School or doing your own research screening stocks and examining the health of a company you may want to own a share in. They consistently trounce the market with educational and amusing advice to their Foolish followers and even some fun contests (count me in!)

If you are interested in starting your own business, you might get some ideas from the book "Cracking the Millionaire Code" by Mark Victor Hansen ("Chicken Soup for the Soul" books) and Robert G. Allen (several best-selling financial books), who are committed to helping others become wealthy, responsible stewards. There are many home-based business opportunities and franchises with new owner education and support.

Resources: (buy them used online or borrow from a library)

"Financial Peace Revisited" Restoring Financial Hope to You and Your Family" by Dave Ramsey © 1992, 1995, 1997, 2003 Viking, Penguin Putnam Inc., 375 Hudson St., New York, NY 10014

"More than Enough" Proven Keys to Strengthening Your Family and Building Financial Peace by Dave Ramsey © 1999 Viking, Penguin Putnam Inc., 375 Hudson St., New York, NY 10014

"The Total Money Makeover: A Proven Plan For Financial Fitness" © 2003, revised 2007 by Dave Ramsey Thomas Nelson Publishers, Nashville, TN – Workbooks available too!

"Money Matters" Answers to Your Financial Questions by Larry Burkett, Crown Financial Ministries © 2001 Thomas Nelson Publishers, Nashville, TN

"Your Money Map" A Proven 7-Step Guide to True Financial Freedom by Howard Dayton, Crown Financial Ministries © 2006 Moody Publishers

"Crown Money Map" Financial Software © 2006 Crown Financial Ministries

"The Motley Fool Money Guide" Answers to Your Questions About Saving, Spending and Investing by Selena Maranjian © 2001 The Motley Fool, Inc., 123 North Pitt St., Alexandria, VA 22314

The Motley Fool's **"You Have More Than You Think"** The Foolish Guide to Investing What You Have by David and Tom Gardner © 1998 by The Motley Fool, Inc., Fireside, Rockefeller Center, 1230 Avenue of the Americas, New York, NY 10020

"The Wealthy Barber" Everyone's Commonsense Guide to Becoming Financially Independent by David Chilton © 1998 Prima Publishing, Roseville, CA

"Money: A Users Manual" Avoiding Common Traps by Bob Russell © 1997 Multnomah Books, Questar Publishers, Inc., P.O.Box 1720, Sisters, Oregon 97759

Websites:
www.daveramsey.com   Dave Ramsey website
www.crown.org   Larry Burkett, Howard Dayton and Crown Financial ministries

www.christianstewardshipnetwork.com	Find Christian counseling near you
www.southeastchristian.org	SECC volunteer financial counselors
www.fool.com	The Motley Fool Financial website
www.southeastchristian.org	Southeast Christian Church website
www.livingword.org	Dave Stone Sermon 1-25-04, online resources
www.nfcc.org	National Foundation for Credit Counseling 1-800-388-2227
www.myvesta.org	Nonprofit consumer education

Section Three – Living the Promise

Chapter 11 – Forgiveness

I've heard it said that forgiveness is God's gift to us to help us live in a world that is not fair.

Dr. David Stoop defines forgiveness as giving up our right to revenge, to perfection and to justice. Instead, we give forth to ourselves and to the offender freedom from the past and an openness toward the future. We cancel the debt of someone who owes us compensation and pardon them from any future retribution.

Now this is not to say that we "forgive and forget" as we have often heard. We retain the right to *remember* the offense, to protect ourselves from any further exposure to the offender, but we give up our right to hold that offense against them. How do parents forget about their children killed by a drunk driver? As Christians, we are commanded to forgive all others, but *reconciliation* is always optional. We give up the right to retaliate against an offender, but we can and should place appropriate boundaries for our safety and protection of others. We can forgive a thief, a sexual predator, even a murderer, but we still lock up our valuables, protect our children and deny freedom to dangerous criminals. Trust, confidence and reconciliation are *always* optional and take time to rebuild. The spouse who has an affair is to be forgiven, but trusting and reconciling may take months or even years, or may never happen at all. If we forget the offense, or fail to place appropriate boundaries after being wronged, we risk allowing repeat offenses and far deeper damage, or enabling multiple victims of the same offender. In some cases, reconciling would not be wise. We forgive, but remember.

Forgiveness is always necessary for there to be any chance of reconciliation, but forgiveness cannot, and should not *guarantee* there will be reconciliation. There will have to be some repentance and work on the part of the offender to try to repair the relationship and rebuild trust. Even forgiveness takes time as there are stages we go through when we are harmed by another person. But we need to take the time necessary for genuine forgiveness. This in no way condones the wrong by forgiving, we will still remember the offense, but we must forgive.

Forgiveness is a solitary activity; I don't need the other person to participate in the process for me to forgive. Reconciliation is a bilateral process, requiring participation of both parties if it is to be successful.

That's how God has forgiven us. He did not involve us in the process, He acted on His own. In the fullness of time, God sent His Son, Jesus, to die on the cross to pay the penalty for *our* sin. He didn't ask us first, He just did it. When Jesus died on the cross, the penalty for every sin that has ever been committed, and ever will be committed, was paid once and for all. God did it all by Himself, without our involvement. NIV Romans 5:8 But God demonstrates his own love for us in this: *While we were still sinners*, Christ died for us.

Why should I forgive? Great question. It is for your own benefit. Forgiveness is the way God resolves the issues of our past, and it is the only way any of us can achieve such resolution. We are never more like God than when we forgive. And no one has forgiven more than God has. Only forgiveness can free the heart from the burdens of the past, releasing us to be what God wants us to be. As long as we hold a grudge against someone and refuse to forgive others, we cannot flourish and grow to be what God created us for. Even secular science has documented health benefits related to forgiveness

Forgiveness heals the heart, research hints: May 20, 1999
Web posted at: 4:00 p.m. EDT (2000 GMT)
From Medical Correspondent Eileen O'Connor

WASHINGTON (CNN) — Littleton. Kosovo. Now Georgia. Never before, say some experts, has there been such a need to forgive what seems to be the unforgivable. Studies funded by the Templeton Forgiveness Research Campaign are trying to monitor and measure the physiological effects of forgiveness and its benefits, taken from the pulpit into the lab.

Everett Worthington is the director of the campaign. One day after mailing off his manuscript outlining a step-by-step process of forgiveness, his own ability was sorely tested when his mother was murdered.

"I remember looking down at the wall and seeing a baseball bat and saying, 'I wish that whoever did this was here right now. I would beat his brains out,'" Worthington said.

Instead, Worthington took his own medicine, focusing on what he considers the most important component of forgiveness — empathy. In this case, for the burglar who killed his mother.

"I can imagine what it must have been like for this kid to hear behind him a voice saying something like, 'What are you doing here?'" he said.

By understanding how it might have happened, Worthington says he's been able to forgive his mother's murderer.

"I cannot imprison him by holding unforgiveness towards him," he said.

Researchers say there is a physiological reason for forgiveness — health.

At Hope College in Michigan, researchers measure heart rates, sweat rates and other responses of subjects asked to remember past slights.

"Their blood pressure increases, their heart rate increases, and their muscle tensions are also higher," said Professor Charlotte van Oyen Witvliet. This suggests their stress responses are greater during their unforgiving than forgiving conditions.

Scientists also find that forgiveness has a lot to do with genetics. Research in chimpanzees shows it might even be crucial for survival of the species.

"In a cooperative system, it is possible that your biggest rival is someone who you will need tomorrow," said Frans De Waal of Emory University's Yerkes Primate Center. End of article.

When we refuse to forgive, it *can cause* illness or disease. An unforgiving heart is very unhealthy. It's like drinking poison and expecting our enemy to die from it. Unforgiveness is like acid, it eats away at its container. Only when it is released are we freed from the negative effects of it. We've all seen the "type A" personality with high stress levels, short temper, guzzling antacids, full of anger and difficult to be around. These people have more weight problems, and are more prone to heart attacks, strokes, cancer and other serious health and relationship risks. They don't forgive or seek forgiveness.

Old Testament teaching considers forgiveness a "burden" for the person who is doing the forgiving, and is only required when the offender repents of his or her offense. This was and is the Jewish teaching on forgiveness. This view teaches that forgiveness is unfair; it is unjust; it defies human logic and reason – unless the offender repents and asks for forgiveness. Forgiveness must be conditional. Islam teaches the same thing – forgiveness is required only in the context of repentance. Indeed, when confrontation and the offender's repentance are *required* for forgiveness, it *does* become a burden.

But Jesus raised the bar for all of us, taking a more radical - and freeing – approach, teaching that forgiveness is a gift of *grace*. Jesus taught that there is to be no limit to the number of times we forgive. We are to forgive and not keep track of how many times we forgive. We are to forgive even in the absence of repentance; forgiveness is now unconditional.

Does this mean everyone is forgiven? Dr. Stoop says "I believe so." Then why will some people spend eternity without God? It won't be because there is some sin that has not been forgiven. It will be because some people have failed (or refused) to be reconciled to the forgiving God. What remains now is for each of us to enter into the reconciliation process with the forgiving Savior. That begins with our showing godly sorrow (repentance) over our sinfulness. We can enter into the process with what God has already done on our behalf and be reconciled, or we can walk away like the servant in the parable – forgiven, but unreconciled to the forgiving savior.

There are three paths we can take when we have been wronged by another person. Two of these paths lead to destruction. The first path is the path of denial, but this only leads to depression as we deny the hurt occurred or (wrongly) blame ourselves for what happened. The second is the path to bitterness, where we obsess over the event and seek the answer to why it happened. We think if we only knew why it happened, we could get over the offense and let it go. But it doesn't work that way. The "why' is never answered to our satisfaction and we cling to our right to revenge and payment, leading to a lifetime of bitterness. Even when we get revenge, maybe we win a multimillion dollar lawsuit, it doesn't lead to healing. Ask anyone who has been there. The best path to take is the path to forgiveness, where we place blame honestly and appropriately, we grieve the loss, we forgive, we *consider* reconciling, if it is appropriate, and we learn to trust again and grow from the experience. We release our feelings of anger, hatred, frustration and payback and learn to love and live again in relationship with safe, healthy people.

One of the most difficult things people face is forgiving themselves. What do we do when we are the offender? And we all are at some point in our lives. We all hurt others, sometimes by accident, sometimes by our negligence or anger. How can I forgive myself when I am the drunk driver that took the lives of others, yet I survived? Dr. Stoop has some help for that too. We read in 1 John that God will forgive us for all of our sins: "NIV 1 John 1:9 If we confess our sins, he is faithful and just and will forgive us our sins and purify us from all unrighteousness." This does not list any exceptions. God will forgive us. Why won't we forgive ourselves? Dr. Stoop might say something to this effect: "I find it interesting that you have higher standards than God does. He can forgive you, but you can't forgive you. How is that possible?"

Anyone who has sinned boldly, or is highly sensitive to sin in his or her life, will struggle with forgiving himself or herself. It is not pride, nor is it weakness, that we accept God's forgiveness *and* hold on to an attitude of unforgiveness toward ourselves. It is a sensitive spirit that holds us back. There are three principles for moving past this. First, don't isolate – place yourself in the presence of those who love you. Second, you need to put yourself in a *place* where you are loved and where you can experience being loved. Third, do something! Get busy doing something meaningful, something God wants you to do. Feel the love of God and the love of others around you. Seek to make amends with those whom you have offended and graciously wait for their response. Create the opportunity for the other person to offer forgiveness without insisting on it. Allow them to forgive on their own timetable. But you forgive yourself after accepting your part of the blame, grieve and be angry for the foolish behavior and experience sadness over the hurt we have caused to others and ourselves. Then forgive yourself unconditionally and never hold it against yourself again. Put boundaries in place to prevent a repeat of the offense and seek reconciliation if it is appropriate. Then you can heal, grow and trust again.

Again, why should I forgive? Dr. Stoop cites a study conducted by Duke University Medical School in which it stated the number one killer in the United States was not cancer, heart disease, AIDS or any of the other commonly cited causes of death. Instead of looking at disease, the researchers looked at attitudes and emotions and found the number one killer in America was a spirit of unforgiveness.

Physical benefits

The researchers were looking at what might be called the "hidden death syndrome" related to unforgiveness. They were saying that, hidden behind heart disease, cancer and the other fatal diseases in our country lies an emotional mind-set of unforgiveness.

What happens to our bodies when we don't forgive? We live in a state of stress, leading eventually to burnout, both physical and emotional. We live with tension and smoldering anger. We might be avoiding someone. We have given control over to others, making us feel helpless and frustrated about our circumstances. When we struggle with these things, various hormones are released into our bodies. One is adrenaline, significant blood levels of which can have serious consequences for the heart, nervous system and immune system when maintained long term. In the early stages, we may experience headaches, muscle tension, fatigue problems with sleeping, digestive problems, ulcers, and depression. If we take the Path of Denial or the Path of Bitterness, and continue to experience elevated blood levels of adrenaline and other hormones associated with chronic anger, our blood pressure could become chronically elevated, we could develop heart disease or we could become more susceptible to cancer. Medical research no longer questions the connection between the attitudes of unforgiveness and chronic low-level anger, and major forms of illness; current research now places greater focus on the *degree* to which these attitudes contribute to these major illnesses.

One study of cancer patients who had been diagnosed as terminal (expected to live six months or less) found that those who completed a special anger-management program – along with traditional medical treatment – were more likely to go into remission than those who only received the traditional medical treatment. In that program, patients were taught different ways to handle their anger and were given specific training in how to move from an attitude of unforgiveness to an attitude of forgiveness.

Long term follow-up of these patients revealed that many experienced remissions from the cancer for a number of years. When the cancer did return, researchers found that this relapse could be correlated with a return to old ways of handling anger and forgiveness. One doctor noted that forgiveness, as taught by Jesus, was the "2000-year-old health tip."

Emotional benefits

In another study, looking at emotional benefits, it was found that empathy and perspective-taking are two skills found in emotionally mature people. Empathy is emotional understanding of the offender, while perspective-taking is cognitive, mental understanding. The better able we are to put ourselves in someone else's shoes, the better the quality of our relationships and our own mental health.

When people forgive a person for a major hurt, they are literally set free. We often believe we are retaining or regaining a sense of power and control when we withhold forgiveness, but that is a false sense of control. We think we are in control, but the truth is quite the opposite. When we forgive, we actually regain self-control when we give up control. This principle was demonstrated by a study of persons who had been deeply hurt by divorce. The researcher found:

> For those people who forgave from the heart, their sense of personal power increased over time. They felt more in control of their personal decisions, finances, feelings and responses to the offender. Those who did not forgive, or who forgave out of fear or out of a desire for personal gain, found that their sense of power *decreased* over time.

Forgiveness restores the belief that we have some power over what happens in our own lives.

Relational benefits

Perhaps one of the greatest benefits we can experience when we forgive is the possibility of a restored relationship. Forgiveness is an essential ingredient for a successful, satisfying marriage and happy successful families. In families where forgiveness is taught by both word and example, negative outcomes are minimized. Forgiveness is the opposite of denial and family secrets, both of which contribute to increasing family problems. Genuine forgiveness never does away with accountability; accountability is a given. Yet genuine forgiveness with accountability in relationships always opens up the possibility of greater levels of trust and intimacy.

Reconciliation in relationships is *only* possible when there has been forgiveness. As we've noted, not every relationship can or should be restored, but when forgiving, we always want to consider the possibility of reconciliation.

Spiritual benefits

How can we be free to worship when we are holding a grudge against someone? We can't. That's why Jesus instructs us,

> NIV Matt 5:23-24 "Therefore, if you are offering your gift at the altar and there remember that your brother has something against you, leave your gift there in front of the altar.

First go and be reconciled to your brother; then come and offer your gift.

If we are harboring a spirit of unforgiveness, we have become co-offenders and need to confess our spirit of unforgiveness and make amends. When we fail to do this, we begin to isolate ourselves, not only from other people, but also from our relationship with God. Our prayers become empty, and we feel hypocritical. The Scriptures are empty of meaning. Other believers irritate us. We become cynical about our faith and life.

When we give up our unforgiving spirit, we experience new freedom in our personal lives and new meaning in our spiritual lives. We don't feel isolated. We are more at peace with our faith and beliefs. We feel like God is there, present in our lives, and we have a wider perspective on all of life that adds meaning to our own lives.

10 Steps to Forgiving from the book "When Your Past is Hurting Your Present" by Sue Augustine

It's all well and good to talk about forgiveness, but how do we do it? If we have chosen to forgive and have decided to do it without looking back, what comes next? Here are some steps to get you started:

1. Make a deliberate decision to stop discussing the story with others. You may need to confide in one trusted friend or a trained professional for therapeutic reasons, but only open your heart to someone you know will encourage you to forgive. Even if you have told others in the past, make a promise to yourself not to talk about it in the future – other than for the purpose of supporting someone else in a similar position. Be uncompromising and strict with yourself. Reject the temptation to keep discussing the story. This is not easy, especially when we are still suffering the pain. If revenge is our goal, we know we can ruin someone's reputation by telling on them with statements like, "Can you believe what she did to me?"

2. Stop mentally dragging up the past. Rehashing hurtful and disturbing scenes over and over again in your mind can drive you crazy. We sometimes do this subconsciously, and other times we keep the anger fresh on purpose, but in either case, we are only hurting ourselves. Besides, the other person has no clue about what is going on inside our heads. We are suffering, yet it's not having any effect on them.

3. Be pleasant and congenial when you are in the company of those you forgive. This doesn't mean you have to go out of your way and conspicuously make an effort to be hospitable or sugary sweet. Simply don't say anything in reference to the event or do something that would cause them to feel ill at ease or apprehensive.

4. Avoid putting anyone on a "guilt trip." Guilt is most painful, and if we are truly ready to forgive, then we won't want others to have feeling of self-reproach, humiliation, or shame. Remind yourself of the Golden Rule – Do to others as you would have them do to you (Luke 6:31). In your mind, say a blessing over them. Mentally give them your consent to break from their own past and move forward.

   One of the reasons others may have a difficult time apologizing or asking forgiveness is that they may have stopped growing – emotionally or spiritually. Pray that they will seek God's forgiveness for themselves and that they will thrive in their spirit, flourishing in every way. The opposite of blessing a person is wishing for his failure, or hoping for disaster to strike. That's when you want his success to be impeded in some way – or you are even hoping for the worst. You will know you have truly forgiven someone when you genuinely want the best in life for him and can sincerely bless him.

5. When a person is remorseful, do what you can to restore a sense of dignity. Allow others to feel good about themselves again by saying whatever you can (if it is true!) to restore their sense of worth, value, and self-respect.

6. Abolish any sense of self-righteousness in yourself. As long as there is even a trace of arrogance or condescension in it, or any finger pointing, your attempt at total forgiveness will not

succeed. Sometimes we can use false "kindness" to try to make the other person feel miserable.

7. Behave as though you don't even think they did anything wrong. This can be most difficult for all of us, but sometimes acting in a certain way helps us to actually experience the feeling. Remember the old phrase, "Fake it 'til you make it"? Actors do it all the time when they have to depict a certain emotion. It's an amazing attribute of human nature. You can act as if you hardly noticed the wrongdoing – and before you know it, the genuine feelings soon come along.

8. Make total forgiveness a lifelong commitment. Once you have chosen to forgive, keep it up today, tomorrow, and forever. Some days will be easier than others. You will have times when you think you have won a complete victory and are totally free from harboring and resentment, then WHAM! – the very next day, something happens to remind you of what someone did and of the utter injustice of the fact they will never be punished or exposed. That old temptation to "go public" or hold onto the bitterness will emerge once again. Not only will you have to make the commitment to forgive, but your pledge will have to be renewed periodically.

    Even if I did not share with others what I was going through, there was a time when I felt justified in going before God and pleading my case. "He ought to be punished", "She doesn't deserve to be let off the hook." Then, when I began thinking of God as my Father in heaven, I realized that, like most parents, He wants His children to get along and love one another. After all, no parent likes it when one child comes squealing on the other, demanding they be punished. But our Father loves all His children equally.

9. Pray for those who have wounded you. That's a difficult one to understand or put into practice. When you pray, be completely honest with God. If you feel angry, tell Him. Say, "Lord, nothing in me wants to pray for this person." Confess your anger, hurt, unforgiveness, resentment, and disappointment. Ask God to give you a right spirit and renewed sense of love. Trust Him to heal the situation. The Bible says, "Let us not grow weary in doing

good, for in due season, we shall reap if we do not lose heart" (Galatians 6:9 NKJV). If you truly want to be set free from a past that is crippling you, desiring the best for your enemies is a powerful step. Something happens to our hearts when we pray for another person. The hardness melts away, and we become able to move beyond the hurts to forgive. Miraculously, we are even able to love the person we are praying for. It happens because, through prayer, we enter into God's presence – and He fills us with His own spirit of love.

10. Ask for healing for yourself. Memories of the situation can come back to haunt you when you least expect it. God's healing will release you from the hurtful recollections and the harmful emotions that go with them.

Forgiveness is getting a lot of good press these days in the secular setting. In counseling, secular therapists and researchers are looking at forgiveness as a powerful therapeutic tool that has very positive effects.

We need to be careful that we do not take forgiveness out of its spiritual context, however, because forgiveness can best be understood only in the context of our being forgiven by God. The theological and spiritual roots of forgiveness are what give it its healing power. Apart from that, forgiveness can be a helpful tool but never to the same degree as when it is connected to the reality of God's forgiveness of us.

God longs for us to be forgiving people. Counselors and pastors are to model forgiveness; families need to model forgiveness as a way of life; couples need to model forgiveness with each other in order to build strong marriages. We can only truly model forgiveness when we ourselves know how to forgive. When we can recognize our own sinfulness and see the universality of sin, we are less likely to develop a condemning spirit. Whenever we experience a deep wound in our souls through the action of another, we have a choice as to which path we are going to take. Pick the Path of Forgiveness. When we forgive, we are giving God the opportunity to work miracles in our lives in His way and in His time. God always honors the move toward forgiveness – it is His plan for us.

NLT Matt 6:14-15 "If you forgive those who sin against you, your heavenly Father will forgive you. But if you refuse to forgive others, your Father will not forgive your sins." – Jesus of Nazareth
We are never more like God than when we forgive.

Resources:
"Forgiving the Unforgivable" Free Your Heart Through Heartfelt Forgiveness by Dr. David Stoop[s] © 2001, 2003 Regal Books from Gospel Light, Ventura, CA

"Forgiving Our Parents, Forgiving Ourselves" by Dr. David Stoop © 1991, 1996 Servant Publications, P.O.Box 8617, Ann Arbor, MI 48107 – Includes Study Guide

"Making Peace with Your Father" Understanding the Role Your Father has Played in Your Life- Past to Present by Dr. David Stoop © 1992, 2004 Regal Books from Gospel Light, Ventura, CA

"I Should Forgive, But…" Finding Release from the Bondage of Anger and Bitterness by Dr. Chuck Lynch © Thomas Nelson Publishers, Nashville, TN

"Happiness is a Choice" 2nd edition, The Symptoms, Causes and Cures of Depression by Drs. Frank Minirth and Paul Meier © 1978, 1994 Baker Books, P.O.Box 6287, Grand Rapids, MI 49516

"The Hiding Place" by Corrie ten Boom © 1971, 1984, 2006 Chosen Books, Baker Publishing, P.O.Box 6287, Grand Rapids, MI 49516 - updated 35th anniversary edition, 2006

"Amazing Love: True Stories of the Power of Forgiveness" by Corrie ten Boom, © 2007 CLC Publications, P.O. Box 1449 Fort Washington, PA 19034

"When Your Past is Hurting Your Present - Getting Beyond Fears that Hold You Back" by Sue Augustine © 2005 Harvest House Publishers, 990 Owen Loop North, Eugene, OR. 97402

"The Freedom and Power of Forgiveness" by John MacArthur © 1998 Crossway Books, A division of Good News Publishers, 1300 Crescent St., Wheaton, IL 60187

"Healing is a Choice – Ten Decisions That Will Transform Your Life & Ten Lies That Can Prevent You From Making Them" by Stephen Arterburn © 2005 Thomas Nelson Publishers, Nashville, TN

Websites:

www.livingword.org   SECC audio and video resources

http://www.newlife.com/nlm/articles.asp   New Life Ministries
                                          resources

www.newlife.com   New Life Ministries (Dr. David Stoop)

1-800-NewLife   Toll Free 24-hour Helpline

Chapter 12 – Raising Great Kids

One of the problems I have with most Christian parenting books is that they tell you how to do everything right from birth to adulthood and, if you don't stray from their advice, your kids will be perfect adults. I think it's great that many authors have had such a wonderful experience, and their kids have grown up to be successful, godly adults, and perfect parents themselves. But the Bible doesn't guarantee this; in fact, it is replete with examples of Godly parents who failed their kids, only to have calamity fall upon future generations. Adam and Eve produced the first murderer, Noah's son was disrespectful, and Abraham's sons were deceitful, as were Isaac's sons and Jacob's sons, who even sold Joseph to slave traders because they hated him. David's sons were incestuous and murderous, and it goes on and on.

I heard a story once about twins of an alcoholic father, one twin became an alcoholic because the father was alcoholic, the other became a teetotaler, because the father was an alcoholic. What's the difference? Why would two kids growing up in the same environment, with the same genetic history and the same parents make such opposite choices? It's all in our attitude toward life and the way we react to the cards we are dealt in life. We can use our history as an excuse for making our own bad choices, or we can learn from the bad choices of others and vow never to treat others in the negative way we have been treated. We can raise our kids by repeating and perpetuating the mistakes of our parents, or we can learn from their mistakes and find a more loving and effective way to deal with the issues of raising great kids the way God intended. He is trusting us with the next generation to guide them into His kingdom. Of course, the choices they make are their own, and even the most godly parents can have ungodly children, but statistically kids stand a better chance of making right choices when they are trained patiently and lovingly in the ways of God.

NKJ Proverbs 22:6 Train up a child in the way he should go, and when he is *old* he will not depart from it. The parable of the prodigal son suggests that he *may* depart from it along the way to becoming old.

The reality is we need advice pertinent to where we are today. We *didn't* do everything right, and now we have a rebellious, out-of-control teenager, or a video game addict. The toddler runs the household with tantrums. We are divorced and remarried with step-children and didn't influence their earliest years. I appreciate the story of Franklin Graham ("Rebel with a Cause"), son of evangelist Billy Graham. We need help for those of us who didn't do it right from the very beginning.

Blended families, those with step-parents and step-children have their own unique challenges. In addition to protecting and providing for the family, new parent-child relationships are being established and there is a delicate balance between love and discipline. The old axiom about "rules without relationship leads to rebellion" is true and the enforcement must be primarily done by the blood parent until the loving relationship is firmly established with the step-child. These five principles have proven successful in both blended and traditional families:

1. Divorce is not an option. Take that off the table from the start and conflict resolution has a better chance of success. Both spouses can be more open when the environment of uncertainty is removed. This fosters mutual trust and is reassuring to the kids.
2. My spouse is my number one relationship on this earth. Not my mother, father, children, siblings or friends, etc. Parents

run the home, parents will be held accountable by God, no one else.

3. Commit to walking in the footsteps of Christ. Do this by studying God's Word personally and in community with other believers and do what it says to the best of your ability.
4. The Word of God is the filter through which all decisions are made. It doesn't matter what all the other kids are allowed to do, our standards are God's standards.
5. Live Psalm 127:1, "Unless the Lord builds the house, the builders labor in vain." Keep God the central focus in your home and in your life, and attend a Bible-believing church for worship.

As of this writing, I am involved in the raising of six children from two months old to 19 years old, fairly evenly spread out 3-5 years apart. My wife and I have not parented perfectly, and it may be 30 years before we know where we have succeeded or failed with each child. There are no guarantees any of them will turn out as we expected, in fact, odds are *none* of them will. But we hope that we have given them all of the basics they need to be strong Christians, knowing they can trust and depend on Jesus no matter what trials and tribulations they may face in life. If I had to condense my job as a parent to a simple description, I would say that my job is to train and coach my children to be good problem solvers, to know that they can do anything within the will of God, and that nothing is more important than their personal relationship with and devotion to Jesus. It is my sincere desire that all of my kids will make decisions for Christ and live the life that Jesus calls us to live. However, I know that kids or young adults are rebellious at times, and that God has given all of us the free will to accept or reject the sacrifice Jesus has made for each of us. Ultimately, I can do no more than to be a role model for them and lead by example, and even that can't be done perfectly. I hope they will learn from my mistakes, limiting their own "hard knocks" and sparing them unnecessary pain from the consequences of their own poor choices. Life is hard enough; let's not make it worse with bad choices. The Bible guides us with timeless wisdom and proverbs we need to learn from and live by.

George Barna lists four areas where children need our help in developing a biblical worldview.

1. Purpose – identifying their purpose in life
2. Perspective – clarifying their core life perspectives
3. Provision – providing basic conditions and benefits they need to grow in a healthy manner
4. Performance – describing the performance of specific activities that enable them to lead productive and meaningful lives

These are some of the best resources that have been helpful in guiding me and my wife through this maze of parenting. I especially recommend starting with the "Boundaries" books.

Resources:
"Transforming Children into Spiritual Champions – Why Children Should Be Your Church's #1 Priority" by George Barna © 2003 Regal Books/Gospel Light P.O.Box 3875, Ventura, CA 93006

"Complete Book of Baby and Child Care" by Focus on the Family Physicians Resource Council © 1997 Tyndale House Publishers, Wheaton, IL 60189

"The Complete Parenting Book" by Drs. David and Jan Stoop © 2004 Fleming H. Revell, a division of Baker Publishing Group, P.O. Box 6287, Grand Rapids, MI 49516

"Helping the Struggling Adolescent – A Guide to Thirty-Six Common Problems for Counselors, Pastors, and Youth Workers" by Dr. Les Parrott III © 1993, 2000 Zondervan, Grand Rapids, MI 49530

"The Most Important Place on Earth – What A Christian Home Looks Like and How to Build One" by Robert Wolgemuth © 2004 Nelson Books, Nashville, TN

"She Calls Me Daddy - Seven Things Every Man Needs to Know About Building a Complete Daughter" by Robert Wolgemuth © 1999 Focus on the Family, Tyndale House Publishers, Wheaton, Il. 60189

"Raising Great Kids – A Comprehensive Guide to Parenting with Grace and Truth" by Drs. Henry Cloud and John Townsend © 1999 Zondervan Publishing House, Grand Rapids, MI 49530

"Boundaries with Kids – When to Say Yes, When to Say No to Help Your Children Gain Control of Their Lives" by Drs. Henry Cloud and John Townsend © 1998 Zondervan Publishing House, Grand Rapids, MI 49530

"Boundaries with Teens – When to Say Yes, How to Say No" by Dr. John Townsend © 2006 Zondervan Publishing House, Grand Rapids, MI 49530

"You Can't Make Me! – But I Can Be Persuaded" Strategies for bringing out the best in your strong-willed child, by Cynthia Ulrich Tobias © 1999 Waterbrook Press, A division of Random House Inc., 2375 Telstar Drive, Suite 160, Colorado Springs, CO 80920

"The Way They Learn: How to Discover and Teach to Your Child's Strengths" by Cynthia Ulrich Tobias © 1994 A Focus on the Family book published by Tyndale House Publishers, Wheaton, Il. 60189

"Every Child Can Succeed: Making the Most of Your Child's Learning Style" by Cynthia Ulrich Tobias © 1996 A Focus on the Family book published by Tyndale House Publishers, Wheaton, Il. 60189

"The New Strong-Willed Child – Birth Through Adolescence" by Dr. James Dobson © 1978, 2004 Tyndale House Publishers, Wheaton, IL 60189

"The New Dare to Discipline" by Dr. James Dobson © 1970, 1992 Tyndale House Publishers, Wheaton, IL 60189

"Bringing up Boys – Practical advice and encouragement for those shaping the next generation of men" by Dr. James Dobson © 2001 Tyndale House Publishers, Wheaton, IL 60189

"How a Man Prepares His Daughters for Life" by Michael Farris © 1996 Bethany House Publishers, 11400 Hampshire Ave. South, Bloomington, MN 55438

"How to Stay Christian in College – An Interactive Guide to Keeping the Faith" by J. Budziszewski © 1999 NavPress, P.O. Box 35001, Colorado Springs, CO 80935

"Ask Me Anything – Provocative Answers for College Students" by J. Budziszewski © 2004 TH1NK, NavPress, P.O. Box 35001, Colorado Springs, CO 80935

"How to Stay Christian in High School" by Steve Gerali © 2004 TH1NK, NavPress, P.O. Box 35001, Colorado Springs, CO 80935

"Preparing Your Son for Every Man's Battle – Honest Conversations About Sexual Integrity" by Stephen Arterburn, Fred Stoeker, Mike Yorkey © 2003 Waterbrook Press., 2375 Telstar Drive, Suite 160, Colorado Springs, CO 80920

"Preparing Your Daughter for Every Woman's Battle – Creative Conversations about Sexual and Emotional Integrity" by Shannon Ethridge © 2005 Waterbrook Press, 2375 Telstar Drive, Suite 160, Colorado Springs, CO 80920

"Successful Christian Parenting – Raising Your Child With Care, Compassion, and Common Sense" by John MacArthur © 1998 Word Publishing, A Thomas Nelson Company, Nashville, TN

"What a Difference a Daddy Makes – The Indelible Imprint a Dad Leaves on His Daughter's Life" by Dr. Kevin Leman © 2000 Thomas Nelson Books, Nashville, TN

"Making Children Mind without Losing Yours – How to bring out the best in your children without letting them get the better of you" by Dr. Kevin Leman © 1984 Fleming H. Revell, Bantam Doubleday Dell Publishing Group, Inc., 1540 Broadway, New York, NY 10036

"Adolescence Isn't Terminal – It just feels like it!" by Dr. Kevin Leman © 2002 Tyndale House Publishers, Wheaton, IL 60189

"Parenting Today's Adolescent – Helping Your Child Avoid the Traps of the Preteen and Teen Years" by Dennis & Barbara Rainey © 1998 Thomas Nelson Publishers, Nashville, TN Family Life Today

"Raising Kids for True Greatness- Redefine success for you and your child" by Dr. Tim Kimmel © 2006 Thomas Nelson Publishers, Nashville, TN Family Life Today

"The Smart Stepfamily- Seven Steps to a Healthy Family" by Ron L. Deal © 2002 Bethany House Publishers, 11400 Hampshire Ave. South, Bloomington, MN 55438

"Raising Children in Blended Families, - Helpful Insights, Expert Opinions & True Stories" by Maxine Marsolini © 2006 Kregel Publications, P.O.Box 2607, Grand Rapids, MI 49501

"King Me – What Every Son Wants and Needs From His Father" by Steve Farrar © 2005 Moody Publishers, 820 LaSalle Blvd., Chicago, IL 60610

"Raising A Modern Day Knight – A Father's Role in Guiding His Son to Authentic Manhood" by Robert Lewis © 1997 Focus on the Family Publishing, Colorado Springs, CO 80995

"How to Be A Hero to Your Kids" by Josh McDowell & Dick Day © 1991 Word Publishing, Dallas, TX

"Discover Your Child's DQ Factor – The Discipline Quotient System" by Dr. Greg Cynamon © 2003 Integrity Publishers, 5250 Virginia Way, Suite 110, Brentwood, TN 37027 – The Phonics Game

"Parenting with Love and Logic – Teaching Children Responsibility" by Dr. Foster Cline and Jim Fay © 1990 Pinon Press, P.O.Box 35007, Colorado Springs, CO 80935 **Money Back Guarantee**

"Home Invasion – Protecting Your Family In a Culture That's Gone Stark Raving Mad" by Rebecca Hagelin © 2005 Nelson Current, Thomas Nelson Publishers, Nashville, TN

"Heaven for Kids – Answers kids will understand" by Randy Alcorn © 2006 Tyndale House Publishers, Carol Stream, IL - All about Heaven!

Audio:
"Instructions not Included" by David T. Moore audio sermon series
"Effective Parenting in a Defective World" by Chip Ingram audio sermon series

Websites:

www.josh.org	Josh McDowell Ministries and resources
www.mooreonlife.com	Moore on Life ministry with David T. Moore

157

www.walkthru.org   Walk Thru the Bible Ministry with Chip
                      Ingram

www.family.org   Focus on the Family with Dr. James Dobson
                      website

www.newlife.com   New Life Ministries with Stephen Arterburn
                      1-800-newlife

www.cloud-townsend.com   Drs. Cloud & Townsend resources

www.fltoday.com   Family Life Today ministry of Dennis
                      Rainey

www.thetotaltransformation.com   James Lehman parenting
                                   program

www.successfulstepfamilies.com   Ministry of Ron L. Deal

www.troubledwith.com   A Focus on the Family helpsite

Chapter 13 – Spiritual Maturity

Once we have made the commitment to follow Jesus and become Christians, our journey is just beginning. God does not expect us just to say we are Christians, get baptized and never give Him another thought. God wants us to begin the process of trusting in Him alone and completely, gradually turning over every aspect of our life to His perfect guidance and going where He leads us. This usually gets us out of our comfort zone and stretches our character growth beyond what we thought we are capable of. God has a way of disturbing the comfortable and comforting the disturbed for His purposes. Proverbs 14 & 16 say, "There is a way that seems right to a man, but in the end it leads to death." We are not to do only what "seems" right because we are easily deceived. Matthew sets our priorities straight in Matt 6:33 "But seek first his kingdom and his righteousness, and all these things will be given to you as well." Michael Youssef paraphrases it "If you are searching for happiness, the only one who will be happy is Satan. If you seek holiness, God throws in happiness as an added bonus!"

Here are "12 Steps to Awareness on the Path of Spiritual Growth" from the book "12 'Christian' Beliefs That Can Drive You Crazy" by Drs. John Townsend and Henry Cloud. These may help describe the process of spiritual growth and maturity:

1. We have the ability to own our problems. This is called confession, which simply means "to agree with." We will never change

unless we confess what is true about our condition. Only when we confess that we are stuck will we begin to work on getting unstuck. Only then can we stop blaming others and excusing ourselves. We can then ask for forgiveness and receive it (I John 1:9).

2. We have the ability to confess our failures to solve our problems. We are powerless to save ourselves. We must come to a place where we say, "God, I have failed in my attempts to change and to get better." We must come to the end of ourselves. We fail mostly because we try to overcome our problems by "acts of the will" or by other self-improvement methods. Yet any attempts to solve our problems by ourselves will fail. Therefore I will boast all the more gladly about my weaknesses, wrote Paul, so that Christ's power may rest on me (2 Cor. 12:9). Stop trying harder. It will only bring you more failure. Sometimes you have to stop trying and wait instead.

3. We have the ability to ask for help from God and others. This is the essence of humility: We recognize that we cannot do it alone. Maybe we can't change our sexual orientation, or stop spending money compulsively, or stop being depressed, or stop an eating disorder - but we can ask God and others for help. Ask and it will be given to you (Matt. 7:7). As James says, God is willing to help us: You do not have because you do not ask God (4:2).

4. We have the ability to continue searching and asking God and others to reveal to us what is in our souls. God's Spirit - and people - can help us to see ourselves as we really are. David asks God in Psalm 139 to show him what is wrong with him, and his request brings to the light the brokenness that needs to be loved, and sin that needs to be forgiven and turned from. In twelve-step language, this is the continuing "moral inventory." We grant God permission to change those aspects of us that need changing.

5. We have the ability to turn from the evil that we discover inside ourselves. In repentance we discover the sick, foul, and evil aspects of ourselves. Then we can say, "I do not want to side with that motive or part of me. I want to be different." When we

are controlling, for example, we can confess it to others and to God. Then as we notice how we control others in our relationships, we can repent and turn from it. Character change comes as we confess our sin, get our real needs met, and repent from the evil that we find comes so naturally. We do not have to feed the evil aspects of our personality. We can begin to loosen our hold on them and let them go. Don't think that this is easy. We enjoy our hatred, our bitterness, our envy. We enjoy lust and deceit. Yet realizing that these sins are ruining our lives can motivate us to give up whatever perverse pleasure we gain from holding on to these sins. We can allow God to meet that need in a healthy way through the love of Him and His people. Giving up some evil aspects of ourselves and connecting instead to love is like trading in one friend for another. It is a death and a birth.

6. We have the ability to find out what needs were not met when we grew up in our family, and then take those needs to the family of God, where they can be met. God says that He sets the lonely in families (Ps. 68:6). Through God's family, His church, we can get our needs met. If we missed some necessary nurturing in childhood, for example, we can take our needy parts to others in the body of Christ and establish supportive connections. God asks the strong to meet these needs (Rom. 15:1). If in childhood we lacked the training and support of a father, we can appeal to those in the body to help us learn and internalize what we did not get growing up. This is the building up of [the body] in love (Eph. 4:13 NASB). We cannot expect God to instantly and supernaturally heal the hurts people have inflicted on us. He heals through His people. Because our hurt comes from relationships, our healing must come from relationships also. Jesus asks His people to be his arms that wrap around each other. Our problem is that we seldom ask.

7. We have the ability to seek out those whom we have injured and, when it is helpful, to apologize, admit our wrong, and ask them for forgiveness. This is called making amends: If therefore you are presenting your offering at the altar, and there remember that your brother has something against you, leave your offering there before the altar, and go your way; first be reconciled to your

brother, and then come and present your offering (Matt. 5:23-24 NASB). The Bible teaches that to have peace with God, we must make peace with each other. We cannot claim to be right with God if we are not doing everything in our hearts to be right with others (I John 4:20-21). A crucial aspect of getting well is purifying our relationships with other people and working hard on treating them well. This fulfills the second greatest commandment, Love your neighbor as yourself (Matt. 22:39).

8. We have the ability to forgive others who have hurt us. Having confessed our sins against God and others and having been forgiven, we can give that same grace to others (Eph. 4:32). In fact, our recovery and well-being is intimately tied to our forgiveness of others. It does us no good to receive grace with one hand and deal out judgment with the other (see Matt. 18:21-35). We need to forgive not just with our will, but from the "heart" (Matt. 18:35), from our whole being. Forgiveness is a deeply emotional process whereby we deal with all our feelings. We must be honest about our hurt and anger and not close our hearts and become callous (Ps. 17:10; Eph. 4:19).

9. We have the ability to develop gifts and talents God has given us. He has given us abilities; we must use them. The difference between the "good and faithful servant" and the "wicked and lazy servant" in Matthew 25 is that the first one invested his talents. How much each servant accomplished didn't matter, but whether he had used what he received. The wicked servant did not even try to use what he had.

10. We have the ability to continue seeking God. God promises that if we seek Him, we will find Him; if we knock, He will open the door for us. He teaches us to persevere in prayer and in seeking the answer we want from Him (James 4:2; Matt. 7:7-11; Luke 18:1-8).

11. We have the ability to seek truth and wisdom. Truth is God's revelation in the Bible and in his creation of how He and His universe works. We can be seekers of what He teaches in His Word and students of the works of His hands. Wisdom is practical, applied knowledge, learned through living life. We must

be intimately involved with living in the world and learning through experience (Heb. 5:14).

12. We have the increasing ability to follow God's example of love. Those who love one another, as He commanded us (I John 3:23) recover. Those who hold on to hatred, revenge, and self-centeredness, do not. Love connects us with others, softens our hearts, decreases our isolation, and matures our soul. Practicing love is the best thing you can do to heal from emotional pain.[t]

Additionally there are these "ABC's of Christian G-R-O-W-T-H" from New Life Ministries:

Spiritual growth results from trusting Jesus Christ. The just shall live by faith (Galatians 3:11). A life of faith will enable you to trust God increasingly with every detail of your life, and to practice the following:

-**G**-o to God in prayer daily. "But if you stay joined to me and my words remain in you, you may ask any request you like, and it will be granted." - John 15:7

-**R**-ead God's Word daily. "And the people of Berea were more open-minded than those in Thessalonica, and they listened eagerly to Paul's message. They searched the Scriptures day after day to check up on Paul and Silas, to see if they were really teaching the truth."- Acts 17:11

-**O**-bey God, moment by moment. "Those who obey my commandments are the ones who love me. And because they love me my Father will love them, and I will love them. And I will reveal myself to each one of them." - John 14:21

-**W**-itness for Christ by your life and words. Jesus called out to them, "Come be my disciples, and I will show you how to fish for people!" - Matthew 4:19 "My true disciples produce much fruit. This brings great glory to my Father." - John 15:8

-**T**-rust God for every detail of your life. "Give all your worries and cares to God, for he cares about what happens to you." - 1 Peter 5:7

-**H**-oly Spirit - Allow Him to control and empower your daily life and witness. "So I advise you to live according to your new life in the Holy Spirit. Then you won't be doing what your sinful nature craves. The old sinful nature loves to do evil, which is just opposite from what the Holy Spirit wants. And the Spirit gives us desires that are opposite from what the sinful nature desires. These two forces are constantly fighting each other, and your choices are never free from this conflict." - Galatians 5:16-17 "But when the Holy Spirit has come upon you, you will receive power and will tell people about me everywhere - in Jerusalem, throughout Judea, in Samaria, and to the ends of the earth." - Acts 1:8[u]

These are tips for spiritual growth from the book "The 10 Building Blocks for a Happy Family" by Jim Burns:

Usually, your children's faith is very dependent on the examples they see at home. In other words, you set the pace of spiritual leadership in your home. If you desire your children to have vibrant spiritual lives, then they need to see an authentic faith lived out in their family. No one expects you to be perfect, but you shouldn't expect them to follow a hypocrite either. Consider the following questions. They will help you evaluate your own spiritual disciplines.

1. How is your time with God? How long has it been since you gave God a portion of undisturbed, uninterrupted time and listened to His voice?

Apparently, Jesus made time with the Father an absolute priority. He spent regular time praying and listening. Mark reveals to us, Very early in the morning, while it was still dark, Jesus got up, left the house and went off to a solitary place, where he prayed (Mark 1:35). Luke tells us, Jesus often withdrew to lonely places and prayed (Luke 5:16). Let me ask the obvious: If Jesus, the Son of God, thought it worthwhile to clear His calendar to pray, wouldn't we be wise to do the same?

I asked one of the busiest women I know how she manages to get so much done in the day. She smiled and showed me her schedule.

It read "6:00 A.M. – 6:45 A.M. Quiet Time." She had let me in on a secret. Her strength and her stamina came from her time alone with God each morning. One of my hobbies is reading biographies of great women and men of the Christian faith. They come in all shapes, sizes, denominations and styles; but the one thing they all have in common is a regular, daily time with God.

2. Do you have a supportive, spiritual accountability relationship?
    Life is difficult, and living out a vibrant, contagious faith is not easy.

I am currently involved in a weekly support and accountability group with three other men. When we first started the group, we talked about politics and sports and only briefly mentioned our faith and family issues. One day, one of the group members opened up to tell us he was struggling with his marriage; and from that day on, it has been a much more focused, supportive and deeper-sharing group.

Some support and accountability relationships use questions like the ones below to make sure they're staying on the right track:

* Have you been with a woman/man anywhere this past week that might appear compromising?
* Have any of your financial dealings lacked integrity?
* Have you exposed yourself to any sexually explicit material?
* Have you spent adequate time in Bible study and prayer?
* Have you given priority time to your family?
* Have you fulfilled the mandates of your calling?
* Have you just lied to me?

3. Do you have a person or a group of people with whom you pray on a regular basis?
    We have found that our involvement with a couples' group from our church has been a wonderful source of friendship, support and sharing of parenting ideas. Our group is made up of five couples who all have children about the same age. We've studied parenting and marriage resources together, as well as other Bible study materials.

I remember a season in my life when I was extremely busy and had little accountability. Cathy challenged me by reminding me I had lots of acquaintances and very few friends. She suggested that I get together with a man at my work named John. I told her John was way too busy to spend any kind of regular time with me, but she kept pressing me to speak with him. We ended up meeting for lunch every Wednesday for over three years until he moved away. Our Wednesday lunch was never structured. We talked, shared our week's experiences, perhaps discussed a problem or two and then prayed together. I loved those times, and they made me a better husband, father and focused Christian. Today, John and I see each other every two months because of distance, and we keep the relationship close through phones calls and periodic visits. Over the years, those times together have become very meaningful.

4. If you are married, do you and your spouse have a regular time with God together?

Most couples I know struggle to spend quality spiritual time together. It is easy to get so distracted with the pace of life that we miss an essential ingredient to building a spiritual relationship with our spouse. Cathy and I have tried almost every kind of devotional time together, but most of our experiments have fizzled. However, we've come across a method that may not sound spiritual enough for some, but it works for us. First of all, we try to pray daily for our kids and for ourselves. Prayer connects us with God and with each other, and it focuses us on the right priority of developing the spirituality of our children. Second, each week we go through a meeting plan that is very conversational and relational – and separate from our Bible study and individual quiet times with God. We work through the list below, and we do not need to prepare ahead of time. We'd rather have our time together in a peaceful setting, but we've been known to hold this weekly meeting while driving, watching one of the children's games or even – when I am traveling – on the phone. We both look forward to our weekly spiritual and relational connection.

Jim and Cathy – Weekly Meeting
* Devotional times for the week
* Greatest joy of the week
* Greatest struggle of the week
* An affirmation
* A wish or a hope
* Physical goals
* Prayer

Our life is a journey right up until we breath our last. We do not know if or when God will intervene. The Bible is our insurance policy, our will and it describes our inheritance. It is said that salvation is just 18" away. That is the distance from the head to the heart. This salvation comes from accepting the sacrifice that Jesus made on our behalf, not due to any good deeds or righteousness of our own. Alistair Begg put it this way: "We do not have to become righteous before we can be declared righteous, in fact we CAN"T! You have to simply acknowledge that you are unrighteous before God, and you can accept the righteousness of Christ on your behalf."

DENNIS TINERINO HELD THE titles of Mr. America, Mr. Universe (three times), and Mr. Natural America. He mastered the world of physical power, but his personal life was out of control. Drugs. Gambling. His own prostitution ring. Before long, Dennis was behind bars, where life was even sicker than life outside.

During the times of his arrests, probations, and sentences, Dennis encountered many who tried to tell him how to be saved from his self-destruction. He avoided them all. Finally a former bodybuilder named Ray McCauley called long distance every week to talk about the Bible, and he did it for months. One day he said, "If you'll pray now, God will change your life."

Dennis later wrote, "I couldn't fight anymore. . .I said, 'Lord, forgive me for everything I have done.'"

A new power entered Dennis's life—the power of God's life changing Spirit. He wrote, "A black cloud lifted from my presence. . .God said, 'Dennis, don't look back. You're a new creation today.'. . .The world deceives you into thinking you have to achieve something to be somebody. I realized my value because Somebody died for me."

- Point To Ponder -

Physical power is virtually useless in matters of faith. It can become a hindrance when we allow ourselves to depend on our own strength instead of relying on the omnipotent God of the universe. Dennis Tinerino needed a new point of view after seeing his personal power vanish into powerlessness. He had gratified his desires in every imaginable way, and he had come up empty. After years of struggle, he was ready to reach out to God. When he did, he was transformed on the inside from weak to strong, from self-absorbed to God-centered. He was a new man living a new life.

- Power Quote -

True power is found in spiritual truth, not in the physical body.

- Scripture -

Ephesians 4:23
Let the Spirit change your way of thinking.

- From "The Power Book" by Stephen Arterburn

Jesus told the Pharisees in Matthew 9:12-13 (NKJ) "It is not the healthy who need a doctor, but the sick. But go and learn what this means: 'I desire mercy, not sacrifice.' For I have not come to call the righteous, but sinners, to repentance."

This is where spiritual growth begins, in admitting we are sinners and recognizing our need for forgiveness. There is only One to Whom we can turn: Jesus of Nazareth! Acts 4:12(NIV): Salvation is found in no one else, for there is **no other name** under heaven given to men by which we must be saved."

Resources:

"How People Grow" What the Bible Reveals about Personal Growth" by Drs. Henry Cloud and John Townsend © 2001 Zondervan Publishing House, Grand Rapids, MI 49530

"12 'Christian' Beliefs That Can Drive You Crazy" by Drs. Henry Cloud & John Townsend © 1995 Zondervan Publishing House, Grand Rapids, MI 49530

"9 Things You Simply Must Do to Succeed in Love and Life – A Psychologist Probes the Mystery of Why Some Lives Really Work and Others Don't" by Dr. Henry Cloud © 2004 Integrity Publishers, 5250 Virginia Way, Suite 110, Brentwood, TN 37027

"Transformation – Turn Your Life Around Starting Today!" by Stephen Arterburn and Dr. David Stoop © 1998, 2006 Tyndale House Publishers, Carol Stream, IL

"The 10 Building Blocks for a Happy Family – Learn to Live, Laugh, Love and Play Together as a Family" by Jim Burns © 2003 Regal Books from Gospel Light, Ventura, CA

Websites:

www.homeword.com — Home Word with Dr. Jim Burns

www.newlife.com — New Life Ministries with Stephen Arterburn 1-800-NewLife

www.cloudtownsend.com — Drs. Henry Cloud & John Townsend resources

www.gty.org — Grace to You ministry with John MacArthur

Chapter 14 – Our Greatest Hope

How can I find myself? Some people claim to have found themselves by exploring the earth, climbing mountains in Tibet, or riding a Harley on the open road. Some seek themselves by challenging their physical limits in triathlons, or altering their state of mind to find some "higher truth." The truth is we were designed to seek God and to know who we are in Christ. There are many paths to God, but only one God. When you seek Him honestly and with all your heart, He will reveal Himself to you. By knowing who God is, knowing your Creator, you can know who you are, what your purpose is, and you can develop a relationship with Him. By meeting with others who are in relationship with Him, you will learn to grow spiritually and to love others as God sees them. This is where you will find yourself; in the Bible and in a Bible-believing congregation in fellowship with Jesus Christ.

Bill Maher has ridiculed the Bible as fiction, laughing about Old Testament claims of some people being hundreds of years old. But if our medical experts can find ways to prevent or cure diseases and slow the aging process, they tell us there is no medical reason why we *can't* live hundreds of years. (Perhaps diseases hadn't "evolved" yet in early human history.) If humans can do this, why should we think it difficult for God? Maher has already concluded that there is no God, but this is a foolish statement, because to *know* unequivocally that there is no God, you would have to understand everything about our entire universe, including how life began and how the universe came about. You would have to know every particle in the universe. You would have to *be* God, which of course, makes the statement false. This is why the Bible tells us "the fool has said in his heart 'there is no God'." It is impossible to know that there is no God, especially when there is a God.

The difference between a skeptic and a cynic is that the skeptic is willing to look at the evidence with an open mind and heart. Not the kind of open mind that will allow any nonsense to fill it, which is just being gullible, but an open mind that objectively looks at the evidence before coming to a conclusion. The cynic has already made up his mind, hardened his heart, and is choosing to attack or ridicule that which he believes is false. Maher is a cynic.

Knowing God's will – It is about having a relationship with God, knowing His likes and dislikes, knowing His character, just like knowing your spouse or best friend. You can know their will in most instances because you know them intimately. If you go to a restaurant with a friend you know well, you might be able to accurately predict what they may or may not order from the menu. If you know they love shellfish and dislike pork, they are more likely to order the lobster instead of the ham. In fact, knowing your friend's likes and dislikes will influence what restaurant you even enter, maybe avoiding spicy-hot food establishments in favor of fresh seafood fare. In this same way, as we gain intimacy with God through His Word and a relationship with Him, we can know places God wants us to go and places He wants us to avoid. We can know how He wants us to interact with others, and how we are to behave. God's general will for ALL people includes understanding our sinfulness in light of God's holiness, understanding our need for redemption, accepting Jesus as Lord and Redeemer, being baptized into Him, loving others and always honoring God. In this way, our sins are forgiven and we can pass this Good News on to others we come into contact with. Jesus is the answer, it is to Him we must turn! The following Bible passages give us insight to the will of God, He WANTS us to know His will for us:

NIV Romans 12:1-2 Therefore, I urge you, brothers, in view of God's mercy, to offer your bodies as living sacrifices, holy and pleasing to God— this is your spiritual act of worship. Do not conform any longer to the pattern of this world, but be transformed by the renewing of your mind. Then you will be able to test and approve what **God's will** is— his good, pleasing and perfect will.

NIV 1 Thessalonians 4:14-22 And we urge you, brothers, warn those who are idle, encourage the timid, help the weak, be patient with everyone. Make sure that nobody pays back wrong for wrong, but always try to be kind to each other and to everyone else. Be joyful always; pray continually; give thanks in all circumstances, for this is **God's will** for you in Christ Jesus. Do not put out the Spirit's fire; do not treat prophecies with contempt. Test everything. Hold on to the good. Avoid every kind of evil.

NIV 1 Thessalonians 5:18 give thanks in all circumstances, for this is **God's will** for you in Christ Jesus.

NIV 1 Peter 2:15 For it is **God's will** that by doing good you should silence the ignorant talk of foolish men.

John 6:35-40 Jesus replied, "I am the bread of life. No one who comes to me will ever be hungry again. Those who believe in me will never thirst. But you haven't believed in me even though you have seen me. However, those the Father has given me will come to me, and I will never reject them. For I have come down from heaven to do **the will of God** who sent me, not to do what I want. And this is **the will of God**, that I should not lose even one of all those he has given me, but that I should raise them to eternal life at the last day. For **it is my Father's will** that all who see his Son and believe in him should have eternal life— that I should raise them at the last day."

NLT Ephesians 6:1-13 Children, obey your parents because you belong to the Lord, for this is the right thing to do. "Honor your father and mother." This is the first of the Ten Commandments that ends with a promise. And this is the promise: If you honor your father and mother, "you will live a long life, full of blessing." And now a word to you fathers. Don't make your children angry by the way you treat them. Rather, bring them up with the discipline and instruction approved by the Lord. Slaves, obey your earthly masters with deep respect and fear. Serve them sincerely as you would serve Christ. Work hard, but not just to please your masters when they are watching. As slaves of Christ, do **the will of God** with all your heart.

Work with enthusiasm, as though you were working for the Lord rather than for people. Remember that the Lord will reward each one of us for the good we do, whether we are slaves or free. And in the same way, you masters must treat your slaves right. Don't threaten them; remember, you both have the same Master in heaven, and he has no favorites. A final word: Be strong with the Lord's mighty power. Put on all of God's armor so that you will be able to stand firm against all strategies and tricks of the Devil. For we are not fighting against people made of flesh and blood, but against the evil rulers and authorities of the unseen world, against those mighty powers of darkness who rule this world, and against wicked spirits in the heavenly realms. Use every piece of God's armor to resist the enemy in the time of evil, so that after the battle you will still be standing firm.

1 John 2:15-26 Stop loving this evil world and all that it offers you, for when you love the world, you show that you do not have the love of the Father in you. For the world offers only the lust for physical pleasure, the lust for everything we see, and pride in our possessions. These are not from the Father. They are from this evil world. And this world is fading away, along with everything it craves. But if you do **the will of God**, you will live forever. Dear children, the last hour is here. You have heard that the Antichrist is coming, and already many such antichrists have appeared. From this we know that the end of the world has come. These people left our churches because they never really belonged with us; otherwise they would have stayed with us. When they left us, it proved that they do not belong with us. But you are not like that, for the Holy Spirit has come upon you, and all of you know the truth. So I am writing to you not because you don't know the truth but because you know the difference between truth and falsehood. And who is the great liar? The one who says that Jesus is not the Christ. Such people are antichrists, for they have denied the Father and the Son. Anyone who denies the Son doesn't have the Father either. But anyone who confesses the Son has the Father also. So you must remain faithful to what you have been taught from the beginning. If you do, you will

continue to live in fellowship with the Son and with the Father. And in this fellowship we enjoy the eternal life he promised us. I have written these things to you because you need to be aware of those who want to lead you astray.

NIV 1 Thessalonians 4:1-8 Finally, brothers, we instructed you how to live in order to please God, as in fact you are living. Now we ask you and urge you in the Lord Jesus to do this more and more. For you know what instructions we gave you by the authority of the Lord Jesus. It is **God's will** that you should be sanctified: that you should avoid sexual immorality; that each of you should learn to control his own body in a way that is holy and honorable, not in passionate lust like the heathen, who do not know God; and that in this matter no one should wrong his brother or take advantage of him. The Lord will punish men for all such sins, as we have already told you and warned you. For God did not call us to be impure, but to live a holy life. Therefore, he who rejects this instruction does not reject man but God, who gives you his Holy Spirit.

Is Christianity exclusive? Are other religions? Is Islam exclusive? Yes, Islam says convert or die. Islam has spread by the sword in every Islamic nation, and Christians and Jews are persecuted as enemies of Islam. Ours is not a god who requires us to sacrifice our sons for him, He has already given the life of His Son for us! It is a carnal god that promises 70 virgins for dying in a "holy war." What kind of promise is that? I'm sure that would be a step down for Hugh Hefner and some others, who may have already reached such a lustful goal. What promise does this "god" have for them, if they can exceed that promise here in their lifetime? What promise is there for women; 70 virgin men? What's wrong with them? But I digress. I want to attain something in heaven not attainable on earth, and Jesus gives us that promise and admonition.

NIV 1 Corinthians 2:9 However, as it is written: "No eye has seen, no ear has heard, no mind has conceived what God has prepared for those who love him" —

Mat 6:19-21 "Do not store up for yourselves treasures on earth, where moth and rust destroy, and where thieves break in and steal. But store up for yourselves **treasures in heaven**, where moth and rust do not destroy, and where thieves do not break in and steal. For where your treasure is, there your heart will be also.

We have sure and better promises from the God of the Bible, the one and only God of the universe, and Christianity is the *only* religion that gives us the certainty of such promises and proof they will be delivered.

Eph 1:13-14 And you also were included in Christ when you heard the word of truth, the gospel of your salvation. Having believed, you were marked in him with a seal, the promised Holy Spirit, who is a **deposit guaranteeing** our inheritance until the redemption of those who are God's possession — to the praise of his glory.

To the Christian, death is not the worst that can happen, in fact, death will happen to almost everyone, if you live long enough! It is *how* you die that makes all the difference. Does a person die in their sin, or does that person die in faith, forgiven and washed clean by the blood of Jesus. We all will enter eternity. Will we enter eternal punishment or eternal glory? For the Christian, death is the end of suffering and the beginning of eternal communion with God, and with intimacy more deeply than is possible in this life.

What about the Jews? There are two types of Jews, spiritual Jews who believe in the Judaic form of worshiping God and genetic Jews who are Jewish by heritage and may or may not believe in worshiping God. Jews are unique in the world, no other faith also has a genetic history. We are not born Roman Catholic, or Lutheran, or Hindu, or Islamic or any other faith, these are all by choice, but genetic Jews are born Jews, regardless of their faith, they can not deny that which is in their DNA. Jews can choose not to follow Jewish faith and religious customs, but they are still Jewish by blood. God has chosen the Jews to be His people, He has promised them a Messiah, and God always keeps His promises. God promised Abraham, Isaac and Jacob (Israel) a homeland, and it will come to pass with their Messiah as King. Jesus is the fulfillment of all Messianic prophecies and He will be returning soon to fulfill those prophecies that still remain. This will be revealed to all Jews at God's chosen time. God will never abandon Israel.

Seeking Wisdom

Knowledge of God is always coupled with wisdom (Proverbs. 9:10). Wisdom does not equal knowledge, but if we know nothing we will not be wise.

The Apostle Paul said "I tell you a mystery..." what is this mystery? He continues with the answer: "We will not all sleep, but we will all be changed—in a flash, in the twinkling of an eye, at the last trumpet. For the trumpet will sound, the dead will be raised imperishable, and we will be changed. For the perishable must clothe itself with the imperishable, and the mortal with immortality. When the perishable has been clothed with the imperishable, and the mortal with immortality, then the saying that is written will come true: "Death has been swallowed up in victory." "Where, O death, is your victory? Where, O death, is your sting?" The sting of death is sin, and the power of sin is the law. But thanks be to God! He gives us the victory through our Lord Jesus Christ. Therefore, my dear brothers, stand firm. Let nothing move you. Always give yourselves fully to the work of the Lord, because you know that your labor in the Lord is not in vain." (1 Corinthians 15:51-58)

Yes, the day is coming when we will be changed, perfected and made immortal. This is our promise and our hope. Only the Bible offers such hope to everyone. *No one is excluded!* We can only exclude *ourselves* by ignoring the truths of the Bible and rejecting the salvation available through Jesus Christ. Christianity is not an exclusive religion at all; Jesus calls each of us to a personal relationship with Him, now and for eternity!

To whom shall we turn? I hope by now we have made it clear. Peter had the correct answer:

(NLT) John 6:68 Simon Peter replied, "Lord, to whom would we go? You alone have the words that give eternal life.

It is Jesus alone who gives us hope when life looks hopeless. It is Jesus who does heal the sick, lame and blind. It is Jesus who has risen from the dead and promises we will too if our faith is in Him. It is Jesus who will make our bodies live again in perfect health. Yes, the blind will see, the lame will walk, the sick will be healed and the dead will rise up and be reunited with loved ones for eternity, if they have put their faith and trust in Jesus. Jesus is the ONLY religious leader who has conquered death, walked away from His tomb. Jesus is our Blessed Hope, Judge and Redeemer. Heaven is what we have to look forward to. Read more about it in Randy Alcorn's book "Heaven." It will explain what we have to look forward to after this life and it is very uplifting! Living in a perfect environment with the God who created us, free from sin, pain, hurt or death, and filled with more than we could ask or imagine – that is the PROMISE we have from God Himself! HE LIVES!

Resources:

"Heaven" by Randy Alcorn © 2004 Tyndale House Publishers, Inc., Carol Stream, IL A biblical view of Heaven.

"Seeking Wise Counsel – How to Find Help For Your Problems" by Dr. David Stoop © 2002 Servant Publications, P.O.Box 8617, Ann Arbor, MI 48107

"Experiencing God – Knowing and Doing the Will of God" by Henry T. Blackaby & Claude V. King © 1990 LifeWay Press, 127 Ninth Avenue, North, Nashville, TN 37234

"Why One Way? – Defending an Exclusive Claim in an Exclusive World" by John MacArthur © 2002 W Publishing Group, A Division of Thomas Nelson, Inc., P.O.Box 14100, Nashville, TN 37216

"God's Plan for the Ages – The Blueprint of Bible Prophecy" by Dr. David Reagan © 2005 Lamb & Lion Ministries, P.O.Box 919, McKinney, TX 75070

"Jesus Among Other Gods – The Absolute Claims of the Christian Message" by Dr. Ravi Zacharias © 2000 W Publishing Group, A Division of Thomas Nelson, Inc., P.O. Box 141000, Nashville, TN 37214

"Knowing God" by J.I.Packer © 1993 InterVarsity Press, PO Box 1400, Downers Grove, IL 60515

"The Tom Papania Story" DVD available at www.tompapania.com

Websites:
www.cityonahillproductions.com   **"H2O"** Video Series with-
                                     Kyle Idleman

www.epm.org	Eternal Perspective Ministries with Randy Alcorn
www.newlife.com	New Life Ministries and resources 1-800-NewLife
www.lamblion.com	Lamb & Lion Ministries with Dr. David Reagan
www.gty.org	Grace to You ministries with John MacArthur
www.rzim.org	Ravi Zacharias International Ministries
www.tompapania.com	Tom Papania Ministry

Endnotes

a   "On the Origin of Species by Means of Natural Selection or the Preservation of Favoured Races in the Struggle for Life", Charles Darwin, 1859

b   http://www.physlink.com/education/askexperts/ae280.cfm

c   "A Brief History of Time", Stephen Hawking

d   "The Perfect Antidote" sermon, Michael Youssef

e   Bob Russell from his sermon series "Essentials for a Happy Marriage" www.livingword.org.

f   "Transforming Children into Spiritual Champions" George Barna

g   "Successful Christian Parenting" John MacArthur, Jr.

h   www.newlife.com

i   www.newlife.com

j   From "Raising Great Kids" by Drs. Henry Cloud and John Townsend, Zondervan, 1999

k   "His Needs, Her Needs", Willard Harley

l   Article by Dick Innes - http://www.newlife.com/0/?libid=140

m   Philip M. Stahl, Ph.D., is a psychologist specializing in high conflict divorce in private practice in Dublin, CA. He conducts continuing education training for psychologists, attorneys, judges, and evaluators who work with these families. He is the author of "Complex Issues in Custody Evaluations" and "Conducting Child Custody Evaluations: A Comprehensive Guide."

n   Article by Gregory L. Jantz - http://www.newlife.com/0/?libid=7

o   Article by Drs. Cloud and Townsend - http://www.newlife.com/0/?libid=8

p   Article by Steve Arterburn - http://www.newlife.com/0/?libid=78

q   "How to Get a Date Worth Keeping" by Dr. Henry Cloud

r   Article by Steve Arterburn - http://www.newlife.com/0/?libid=29

s   "Forgiving the Unforgivable" by David Stoop, Ph.D. Copyright © 2001, 2003 by Regal Books, Ventura, CA 93003. Used by permission.

t   Article by Drs. Cloud and Townsend - http://www.newlife.com/0/?libid=99

u   Article by New Life Ministry - http://www.newlife.com/0/?libid=90

Printed in the United States
200007BV00003B/166-249/A

9 781602 666597